T0294621

CULTIVATING PERSONAL AND ORGANIZATIONAL EFFECTIVENESS

Spiritual Insights from African Proverbs

Chiku Malunga

Foreword by Margaret J. Wheatley

University Press of America,® Inc.
Lanham · Boulder · New York · Toronto · Plymouth, UK

Copyright © 2013 by
University Press of America,® Inc.
4501 Forbes Boulevard
Suite 200
Lanham, Maryland 20706
UPA Acquisitions Department (301) 459-3366

10 Thornbury Road
Plymouth PL6 7PP
United Kingdom

Library of Congress Control Number: 2012950274
ISBN: 978-0-7618-6028-0 (clothbound : alk. paper)
eISBN: 978-0-7618-6029-7

I dedicate this book to the global family of individuals committed to creating a better world than they found it through their different endeavors.

Contents

Foreword

Reweaving Ourselves, Reweaving the World

It has been a great blessing in my life to be intimately engaged with South Africa and Zimbabwe since 1995. I often tell my friends and colleagues that if I had not worked in Africa, I would never have discovered what it means to be fully human. Nowhere else have I ever experienced the simple joy that we humans feel because we are together, even in the midst of life's greatest tragedies. I remember so many times when a group I was with transcended their grief and despair by breaking into song. Suddenly, we were together, metabolizing our grief, converting our raw and tender energy into harmonies of triumphant expressions. In these moments, we were calling forth our human spirits, which always lifted us above the dramas and despair of our lives.

Working mostly in Western countries, I've sat in too many meetings with colleagues where we were using only our brains to find our way through a dilemma or crisis. As we talked and argued, our energy dissipated and fatigue and overwhelm took over the room. At these moments, remembering Africans, I wanted to stand up and start singing. I wanted to reconnect with my spirit, not just my tired, depressed brain. But of course I couldn't do that without risking embarrassment and ridicule. Business people don't do such things! And so we labored on, not getting anywhere, while I sat there dreaming of a different experience, wishing I was with Africans.

I believe, as Steve Biko so beautifully said, that "in the long run the special contribution to the world by Africa will be in the field of human relationships." The Western world has denied the value of relationships, discounting the most essential element of life. In the past century, Western science has proven what indigenous people never forgot, that nothing living lives alone, that we are intimately interconnected in the web of life. I've taken great satisfaction in bringing the learnings from modern science to Africans and other indigenous peoples, because the science validates their traditional wisdom and ways.

Western management and development have denied relationships and told ancient peoples they need to become modernized, but in fact what is needed is just the opposite. Western people need to recognize that, as Albert Einstein said: "A human being is a part of the whole, called by us 'Universe,' a part limited in time and space. He experiences himself, his thoughts and feelings as something separate from the rest—a kind of optical delusion of his consciousness. The striving to free oneself from this delusion is the one issue of true religion. Not to nourish it but to try to overcome it is the way to reach the attainable measure of peace of mind."

The work of this time is to reweave the world back to its essential wholeness. Western ways, for 500 years now, have split people into separate and competing capacities: brain versus heart, reason versus intuition, individual versus group, analysis versus compassion, intellect versus spirit. This terrible split has separated us from each other, and divided us internally. We have a hard time remembering what it feels like to be fully functioning, whole human beings. We have forgotten that we are spiritual beings having a human experience.

Reconnecting with the fullness of our human spirits is the path forward into healing: healing ourselves, our communities and our planet. The word for health has an important teaching for us. "Health" comes from the old English word for "wholeness" and wholeness comes from an older word for "holiness." We cannot be healthy until we experience our unity, and until we experience unity, we cannot experience our holiness. The Bible teaches this as well: "Whenever two or more are gathered, there will I be also." We can only experience the sacred if we are together, in genuine relationships.

I am grateful for Chiku's work and this book in particular. From his own spiritual journeying, he offers us great guidance for how we can reweave the world into wholeness inside ourselves and inside our organizations. This is the path forward for us now, using the ancient wisdom of Africa to shine light on the journey ahead.

Margaret J. Wheatley, author of *Leadership and the New Science: Discovering Order in a Chaotic World.*

CHAPTER 1: THE HUMAN SPIRIT IN PERSONAL AND ORGANIZATIONAL DEVELOPMENT

The human spirit is the missing link or ingredient in most personal and organizational development (OD) efforts or initiatives. This is despite the truth that *the body of a person is small compared to the spirit that inhabits it.* Overemphasis on the "power of the mind" has eclipsed and strangled the knowledge and role of the human spirit. Rediscovering the human spirit involves gaining an understanding of spirituality as a discipline and a practice. While spirituality is a very complex phenomenon, it is not too amorphous to the extent of meaning everything and therefore nothing. Spirituality simply means human conduct as it is influenced by the human spirit. Spirituality is about consciousness in the human spirit and how this influences and directs activities at the mental and physical levels.

If spirituality can be defined in one word it is *relationships*—relationship with oneself, others and nature. The message of spirituality is that nothing, absolutely nothing, is more important than people and relationships. Human beings are human because of their relationships, both divine and human. This is the simplicity and complexity of human life. The concept of *ubuntu*, a Bantu word, which simply means "human beings are human because of other human beings," is Africa's spiritual gift to the world. Steve Biko rightly observed when he said, "We believe that in the long run the special contribution to the world by Africa will be in the field of human relationships. The great powers of the world may have done wonders in giving the world an industrial and military look, but the great gift still has to come from Africa—giving the world a more human face (Biko, 2006: 51).

African culture is a people or relationship centered culture. We believe that *hospitality is a form of worship* and that *mutual gifts cement a relationship.* Ubuntu comprises five relationship and people principles (Malunga, 2009: 3 – 9). These are sharing and collective ownership of opportunities, responsibilities, and challenges; the importance of people and relationships over things; participatory decision making and leadership; loyalty; and reconciliation as a goal of conflict management and resolution.

Ubuntu emphasizes that *a home is a home if it is visited, to be without a friend is to be poor indeed, relationships are strengthened by eating together; a roaster may belong to one household but when it crows, it crows for the whole village,* and most importantly that *every relationship is a gift of the Spirit.*

The five ubuntu principles presented above are congruent with the OD people values. According to Hanson and Lubin (1995: 33) some representative OD people values include:

People are basically healthy, self-motivated organisms who need to work and live in systems that respect them and their humanity.

People will support what they help create. They will be more highly interested and committed if they participate in decision making and solving problems that affect their lives both in the community and at work.

People have growth needs that develop from infancy to maturity. These dimensions move from passivity to activity, dependence to independence, simple to complex behaviors, short term to long term perspectives, subordinate position to equal or superordinate position; and lack of self-awareness to self-awareness and self-control.

The growth needs are activated by a certain amount of psychological energy that exists in all individuals, and they will find some type of expression even when they are blocked. When not blocked or thwarted by community and organizational practices or norms that inhibit them, these growth tendencies will facilitate the development of a healthy mature and self-actualizing individuals.

From the OD people values, it can be concluded that OD is essentially about people and relationships and therefore spiritual in nature.

All true personal and organizational effectiveness is based on harmonious relationships as the African proverb, *life is in community,* asserts. For this reason, personal and organizational effectiveness are essentially spiritual in nature. The ability to help individuals and organizations surface, identify and confront their contradictions or shadows for deeper and lasting change is only possible when the relationship between the intervener and the intervened share a healthy, harmonious, and mutually respectful relationship—when each is accepted and respected at the physical, mental, and spiritual levels.

In addition to relationships, spirituality is also about effectiveness. It is about surfacing, identifying, and confronting one's and others' contradictions or shadows constraining effectiveness. A central message of personal and organizational development is that the future is ours to create, that everything is possible if we care enough; and that people should be allowed and encouraged to use their initiative (Handy, 2006: 56).

Lastly, spirituality is about choice or the freedom to choose, and taking responsibility for the consequences of the choices we make, whether those consequences are good or bad. The old African story below illustrates this point well:

Once upon a time there lived a very old and very wise woman. Her fame was so great that people came from all over the world to experience her wisdom. One day two mischievous young women decided to play a trick on the wise woman, to test whether she was truly as wise as she was reputed to be. They arrived at her compound and sought an audience with the famed wise woman. One of them carried her hand behind her back and in that closed hand was a very small bird. 'Tell us, O wise one,' she said, 'I carry in my hand a bird. Is the bird dead, or is it still alive?'

It was a very tricky question. If the wise woman said, 'it is alive' the young woman would only have to squeeze the bird to death. If she said it was dead, she would simply open her hand and let the bird fly away. The wise woman kept silent for a long time just staring at the young women with a kind of sorrow in her eyes. At last she said, 'My daughters, it is whatever you wish it to be.' (adapted from Denis Scott in *Faith for Daily Living* Number 448 – January/February 2010).

By our choices as individuals and organizations, our lives will be "whatever we wish them to be." The choice is in our hands. It is the ability to make conscious choices that sets humans apart from all other creation. The freedom to choose is a fundamental spiritual principle.

In summary, spirituality is about relationships, effectiveness, and choice. It is about cultivating synergistic relationships, consciously working toward realizing developmental goals and making the right choices and decisions based on the information one has.

The rise of spiritual consciousness

There is a general evolution of consciousness that is giving spirituality increasing recognition and acceptance worldwide. Spirituality has moved beyond the confines of religion and is receiving increasing acceptance in the "secular" world. An increasing number of individuals and organizations are making efforts to integrate reason and faith or mind and spirit into their personal and organizational lives (James, 2004). In the words of a high-ranking Russian official a few years ago, "No society has been as well educated in atheism as you find in the USSR...however we have observed that some positive development can be seen in human potentialities as an apparent result of religious roots. Without such roots we may be less than our potential. We are therefore taking a new look at religion" (Schuller, 2001: 435). Indeed, *man's quest is to penetrate the mystery of life.*

Reasons that are leading to an increase in interest in spirituality include:

- Increasing insecurity and uncertainties in the world are forcing more and more people to rethink the meaning of life and whether real security can be attained in the material world alone. Anxiety and stress levels are very high in many parts of the world. People are looking for ways to attain and maintain balance. Spirituality is one of the avenues that an increasing number of people are exploring and turning to.
- In the developed nations of the world, an increasing number of people are finding an "emptiness of affluence" and are looking for meaning beyond material possessions. This is further aggravated by the breakdown of traditional institutions such as the family, and marginalization of religion in personal life. In poor countries, due to increasing and persistent levels of poverty, a large number of people may be turning to spirituality as an escape from the harsh realities of their lives. In this case, spirituality may be wrongly understood and become part of the problem rather than the solution.

In organizational life the reasons include:

- Failure of the majority of organizational change efforts, leading to a search for more innovative and deeper solutions. Change efforts that depended purely on reason and that ignored the invisible or intuition generally did not do well. In his 1995 book, *The Collected Papers of Roger Harrison*, the author states that, "I have never in all my years as a consultant seen anyone change an organization in any fundamental way through rational planning *only*" (p. 163). Ignoring the invisible or spiritual world has been identified as a major reason for the failure of many organizational change efforts.

- Advances in the natural sciences are showing that the world or the universe is one indivisible whole with complex interrelated relationships. This is also contributing to the interest in spirituality. Spirituality is being recognized as part of the process of human evolution enabling human beings to connect the visible and the invisible. Quantum physics, cybernetics, chaos theory, cognitive science, Eastern and Western and African spiritual traditions are shedding more light on the spiritual dimension of life. There is no hard and fast demarcation between the spiritual and the secular as life is one indivisible whole. The African proverb wisely asks *what is not sacred?*

Two months before I turned 40 in October 2011, I embarked on a reflection of the role of spirituality in professional life, especially in my own life. I soon discovered that this was a very lonely journey and often the road less traveled. My aim in this book is to share some of my reflections with fellow travelers, both those who are traveling toward and beyond the 40-year mark, on this spiritual journey of self-discovery.

To the conscious individual, something happens around the middle of their lives. Carl Jung captures it well when he wrote:

> From the middle of life onward, only he remains vitally alive who is ready to die with life. For in the secret hour of life's midday the parabola is reversed, death is born. The second half does not signify ascent, unfolding, increase, exuberance, but death, since the end is its goal (Hyde and McGuiness, 2005: 169).

Steve Jobs put it more strongly and positively when he said:

> Remembering that I will be dead soon is the most important tool I have ever encountered to help me make the big choices in life. Because almost everything—all external expectations, all pride, all fear of embarrassment or failure—these things just fall away in the face of death, leaving only what is truly important. Remembering that you are going to die is the best way I know to avoid the trap of thinking you have something to lose. You are already naked. There is no reason not to follow your heart (Steve Jobs, 2005 quoted in the *Nation* on Sunday, October 9, 2011).

It is at this stage in one's life that the questions below come into sharp focus:

- What will my contribution be? How do I want to be remembered?
- What are the most important lessons I have learned about life so far?
- What are my greatest regrets?
- What is my biggest concern for the world and its future today?
- What is my message to this and the next generation?
- How will my responses to the above questions shape my priorities from now on?

It is lack of consciousness about these questions that may have given rise to the popular maxim "a fool at 40 will be a fool forever."

The journey traveled so far

I made a commitment to development work at the age of 24, soon after graduating from university with a degree in agriculture majoring in rural development. I decided to dedicate my professional life to helping people improve their lives—especially the disadvantaged people. I was fortunate to have as a very strong foundation for my professional career. I underwent a two-year "Organization Development (OD) Practitioner Formation" program that combined European, American, Asian, and African input. The key contribution the program made to my life was that it made me a "thinking and reflective practitioner." A key emphasis was on the role of the "self" or "self-consciousness" as tool for one's own and others' change or development processes. With this in mind, I undertook, for this book, to reflect on two streams in my life: the development of my OD practice and the development of my spiritual consciousness.

I was fortunate to be born in a non-religious home as this gave me an unbiased start in life. My first conscious spiritual encounter was in 1986 when I was 14 years old. I had what evangelical Christians call the "new birth" experience by which is meant a conscious connection with Christ to start an eternal spiritual relationship with Him. I also had what the Pentecostal and Charismatic Christians call the "Baptism in the Holy Spirit" experience by which is meant being equipped for spiritual service. In the same year I made a decision to be baptized in a Christian church. When asked what my religion is I prefer to call myself a follower of Christ—I take Christ as my model of love and service relevant for both personal and professional life. Christ gives me the Spirit, *ubuntu* gives me the strategy, and life gives me the experience.

I have always been aware of the two streams in my life—the professional and the spiritual. I always had a feeling that the two can and should be integrated to create synergy and add value to each other.

Spirituality is an immensely vast and complex subject. One can only contribute in the light of their personal experience. A common feature in most spirituality thinking is the existence of a Power higher than the human self, a First Cause or a Higher Intelligence.

My world view is influenced by the Judeo-Christian cosmology in which the existence of God is taken as a given. I am therefore of the panentheism persuasion. Panentheism is the belief that the being of God permeates and includes, but is not synonymous with, the universe as compared to pantheism—the belief that God and the universe are identical (Carr, 1991: 64).

The questions I had for reflection on the role of the human spirit in personal and organizational development included:

- What is spirituality?
- How does spirituality add value to professional or organizational life?
- What are the stages of spiritual development in an individual?
- How does one cultivate spirituality in one's life?
- How does one integrate the two streams of spiritual development and professional development?
- What are the disciplines and practices that can assist one in seeking and appreciating more of the invisible forces that shape our world?

The challenge of spirituality

Peter Drucker observed that in the modern society of enterprise and management, knowledge is the primary resource and society's true wealth (*Harvard Business Review* 2006: 183). Our boundaries of operation are circumscribed by our type and level of knowledge. Much of our knowledge in understanding human beings today is biological and psychological in nature. This is the type of knowledge that is a component of most formal learning. Spirituality has generally been left to religions. Unfortunately, the religions may not have adequately clarified the difference between spirituality and religion. For a long time, spirituality has been ignored in organizations because it has been mistaken for religion. There is a general ambivalence toward religion among people and in organizations because, according to James (2010: 257), religion has been perceived as being:

- divisive—a rallying point for division and conflict;
- regressive—maintaining and sometimes promoting historical injustices such as slavery, colonialism, apartheid, and ongoing caste and gender inequalities;
- irrelevant—organizational management is seen as an autonomous technical discipline about which "other worldly" religion has nothing valuable to say;
- insensitive—exported in culturally inappropriate ways; and
- proselytizing—seeking to convert others to a particular faith in a coercive way.

The case for spirituality in personal and organizational development

In this book, I assert that a general lack of clear and practical knowledge of spirituality constrains human potential, leaving the world poorer. My years of practice as a development practitioner have taught me that minus spirituality, physical and psychological interventions are often insufficient in effecting fundamental change needed to create truly developmental shifts. Minus spiritual insight, physical and psychological knowledge alone may not go deep enough to effect real change. This is a key explanation of the failure of many change efforts. A major problem observed in many individual's and organization's lives today is captured in the proverb, *"too much knowledge obscures wisdom"* or too much knowledge but less corresponding practice. Without spiritual insight and power, it is difficult to identify, surface and confront one's contradictions. It is difficult to confront one's shadows.

By going through this reflection, my aim in this book is to present a case for spirituality. I submit that spirituality is crucial for maximizing individual and collective human potential. I differentiate between spirituality and religion and assert that spirituality is higher than religion while acknowledging that religion has its rightful place in human existence.

Much of what is taught for spirituality today is too complex and mysterious for an ordinary person to grasp. I aim to present the complex subject of spirituality in a simple enough language that anyone who wishes to can learn and understand. I wish I could entitle the book, "Spirituality Made Simple" but this could not capture the essence of the book, which is to show:

- There is a spiritual dimension to life.
- Spirituality is about relationships of both "person to person" and "person to Person."
- Spirituality can and does add value to personal and professional or organizational life.

According to James (2011: 6) personal and organizational change is more likely to happen if we take a thoroughly professional approach and integrate it with faith. People are spiritual beings. Therefore, if we are to help organizations to change, we should integrate a spiritual dimension as well. *A land is a land because of its people* meaning that an organization is an organization because of its people and therefore the people must be taken and treated as such taking into account their wholeness—body, mind and spirit.

Below are some comments by students who had just finished a course on Spirituality at the Center for Spirituality at the Workplace at St. Mary's University in Nova Scotia, Canada:

> I plan on having a career in the human resources field and I feel as though this course has made me become more aware and sensitive when helping or focusing on employees. I have learned I must take into account the different views and attitudes toward the workplace environment.

> I have become more aware of myself because of this course.

> By knowing and understanding the true meaning of spirituality in the workplace it will allow me to handle human resource problems in a better way.

I have found that spirituality in the workplace has made me a better co-worker.

I have found my calling and I owe it to this class... thank you!

The central message of this book is that neither reason nor faith; neither mind nor spirit, alone is sufficient. The world is moving into the age of integration, which gives room to both reason and faith. In the words of M. Scott Peck (1997) we need a "both/and" thinking. The aim is not to get rid of reason or to revert to the dark days of blind loyalty to faith, but to promote, "reason plus": Reason and mystery. Reason and emotion. Reason and intuition. Reason and revelation. Reason and wisdom. Reason and love. In short, we need, in our personal and organizational lives, to move beyond the age of reason alone to one in which spirituality is given the space to make a more conscious contribution to human progress.

CHAPTER 2: WORK AND THE HUMAN SPIRIT

Introduction

Spirituality is ultimately being conscious of one's responsibility in or to life. The spiritual person understands that he or she is living for a purpose, and that the meaning of his or her life is in that purpose. The purpose is not to be actualized in words but in action or doing. This is concretized in the sense of a mission. The person is not called to do everything or many things. One is called to accomplish one's mission by walking in the path ordered by destiny. For this reason, one's work is to express one's uniqueness and singularity, and in that sense one is not in competition with anyone (Frankl, 1985).

One's work is usually the arena through which one's purpose and meaning of life are channeled. It is through work that contributions to society are channeled. Meaning can also be derived through human or social relationships and enduring unearned suffering, but it is primarily through work that one gets a sense of purpose. This is why unemployment or oppressive conditions of work create such serious psychological and spiritual effects in an individual. Many people who do not handle retirement well, or even redundancies, do not live long. This is because they lose their sense of purpose and usefulness. The feelings of being useful and needed are deep human needs.

It is not so much the occupation or type of work that matters. All occupations and all types of work have a potential to give one meaning. It is not the work itself, but how one views it. The meaning and uniqueness are not derived from the work, because everyone else who is trained in that field can do it. It is in the way one does the work, whether or not one brings one's uniqueness into it. This is what gives meaning to the individual and the people he or she is serving. Patients will prefer a particular doctor not because she gives different medicine, but because of the way she handles them. Children in kindergarten will prefer a particular teacher not because he teaches different things from the other teachers, but because he makes them feel useful and needed. People will remember a particular presenter from a conference not because she presented different material from the others, but because of the way she made them feel. People will remember a particular musician not because he sings different songs, but because of the way he connects with the audience. It is the spirit behind the activity that matters.

From my experience, I can only talk of my field, organization development. Organization development practitioners basically do the same things. They conduct organizational self-assessments, design interventions, facilitate organizational improvement interventions, including establishing reflection and learning systems aimed at improving organizational consciousness. It is when one goes beyond these activities and brings one's uniqueness and singularity to the task that one can connect with the people in the organization at a deeper and spiritual level. This is what will make a person's work unique and it will bring meaning both to the individual and the client. This is irreplaceable.

It is also important to emphasize that work is part of life and not life itself. Spirituality emphasizes embracing the whole of life and not just parts of it.

There are people who are too busy making a livelihood at the expense of life itself. When my daughters were very young, a female friend told me a story about her father and her. She said her memories of growing up as a young girl were that her father was always away from home. When he was around, he would always carry work from the office. Her memories were of her longing for the father's attention and love. But the father was too busy. She said she remembered crying for the father every time he left until one day at the age of six she told herself that crying for him doesn't help. That was the last time she cried for him. Now she is in her 20s and her father has retired. Now, with nothing much to do, he has all the time in the world. He constantly calls her wanting to spend some time with her. But the problem is that she is now a grown up young lady, and the father's time has passed. This is time for other men in her life, not him. There are no rehearsals in life, and one cannot postpone life. Either you use the different stages you pass through or lose them forever. The child who cries for you when you leave her at kindergarten will one day stop crying for you, and that chapter is closed forever and cannot be reopened.

Life and learning

It is important to emphasize that meaning can be found not only in work but also in love and unmerited suffering. This encompasses the whole of life. The ultimate aim of life is to learn—to learn for this life and to learn in preparation for eternity. We learn through our achievements, by interacting with other humans and nature, and through our sufferings. In this sense, we cannot talk about learning without talking about consciousness. Learning happens where people are aware or conscious. People may accomplish the same achievements. They may undergo similar experiences, or they may go through similar sufferings. But only the conscious will be able to detect or identify the lessons and use them to their benefit. Those who are not conscious will come out on the other end the same way they went in. This is why it is said that many people "sleepwalk" through life. I remember how enthusiastic I used to be in telling others to read a book that I had just finished and felt that it changed me. Sometimes I would almost cram the book down their throats. I would be very lucky if any of them would actually read it. If they did, some of them would wonder what the big deal was. The book could not "speak to them" the same way it spoke to me.

Simply defined, development is the awakening of consciousness. This applies to all levels of human existence—from the individual, to organizational, community, national, continental and global. How well are we learning the lessons life is throwing on our path? The difference between poor and rich countries is usually the difference in levels of consciousness and thinking among the populace. Rich countries are able to learn from their successes and failures and move forward. Poor countries, for one reason or another, fail to learn from their successes and failures, and therefore remain stuck. The bigger the challenge faced, the more consciousness is required to address it. Challenges like climate change, the HIV and AIDS pandemic and persistent poverty are a real test to the global consciousness of the human race.

Life will keep making new demands. When one makes achievements and develops new competencies, life will throw new responsibilities onto one's path. As long as there is life, there is responsibility.

Sowing and harvesting
Judge each day not by its harvest but by the seeds you sow into it

In discussing work from a spiritual point of view, therefore, I deliberately concentrate on taking responsibility. I present some reflective thoughts from my own practice on the primacy of taking responsibility as a key foundation for personal and organizational effectiveness. A key concept I would like to introduce is "surfacing and confronting contradictions." Taking responsibility for organizational and practice effectiveness often means the ability to "surface and confront our contradictions" as individuals, organizations, communities and even countries.

Each seed produces its own kind. The harvest is a reflection of the seeds that were sown. If we are happy with the harvest, we will sow more of the same seeds. If we are not happy with the harvest, we need to change the seeds we sow. Linking harvest and seed is a rare skill in personal, family, organizational or even national life. People get caught up in celebrating the harvest of success, forgetting what produced that harvest in the first place. They get caught up with complaining about the harvest of failure, forgetting or not acknowledging what produced the harvest of failure in the first place.

A key to developing oneself, one's organization or one's community is to take a reflective stance. Such a practice enables people to consciously link the results they are observing to their causes or the seed sown. It enables one to *judge each day not by its harvest but by the seeds you sow into it*. This practice enables corrective action in the case of a wrong harvest. It also enables improvement to bring about a desired harvest. In short, it makes concentration for success possible—concentration of the resources of money, time and energy. Judging each day not by its harvest but by the seeds we sow into it forces us to focus on what happens inside rather than what happens outside, because what happens outside is merely a reflection of what happens inside us. It forces us to focus on our *being* more than our *doing*. It helps us to confront and bring to the surface contradictions between what we truly want and what we are. It helps us to take responsibility for the results we are producing.

For development to take place, people must change behavior, and this requires them to become aware of and then confront the contradictions in their past and current behavior. Just as *when you point a finger of blame at another, the remaining four are pointing back at you*, individuals, communities, organizations and nations must avoid externalizing the problem as "someone else's fault" or "someone else's duty to assist" and begin to take responsibility for their contributions to the current context of problems. When asked what their development problems are, people will usually produce long lists of problems, but they will rarely include themselves as a problem in the lists. But often, the man in the mirror is the biggest culprit; as has been said, *you are the only problem you will ever have and you are also the only solution.*

A "responsibility-based approach" to development is essential if we are to release the will and energy to change. This book, written from the receiving end of a plethora of many development innovations and fashions developed in America and Europe, argues that development only occurs when people, communities, organizations and nations confront their contradictions and take responsibility for doing something about the problem themselves. It argues that development occurs when *people begin to judge each day not by its harvest but by the seed they sow into it.*

Realities of change

A young man recently came to an HIV clinic in Zimbabwe where a friend of mine, Carol, works. When his voluntary test came out negative, he was obviously relieved and delighted. So Carol asked him: "What will you do to remain negative?" He replied: "I will be faithful to my wife at all times, even though she lives in the village while I stay in town. But if 'nature comes' I will always use a condom." He then asked for a packet of condoms. Carol congratulated him for his resolve, but instead of giving him one packet she gave him two packets of condoms. He was surprised, and asked: "What is the other packet for?" Carol replied: "It is for your wife. Take it and give it to her to use when 'nature comes' on her also." The young man looked confused and asked my colleague to repeat what she had said. He went out of the clinic leaving both packets of condoms behind. A few days later he reappeared at the clinic beaming, this time together with his wife who was now staying with him in town. He said to Carol: "We have come to thank you for what you said to me. It had never occurred to me that my wife has a 'nature' too. After leaving your clinic I went home to the village and made arrangements for my wife to join me living in town."

My wife told me a story of a friend whose husband was threatening to stop making public appearances with her unless she lost considerable weight. She tried to lose weight until she couldn't lose any more, but the husband was still not impressed. When she realized that she could not lose any more weight, the wife began to think of ways to make her husband change his mind. She came up with a brilliant idea. She told her husband that she too would only make public appearances with her husband if he regained his lost hair or if he reversed the balding process, which was advancing at a very fast rate. This brought the husband's unrealistic demand to an end.

These stories illustrate, at an individual level, the development process of confronting your contradictions in order to change. This same process is repeated at a community, organizational, national, and even international level. For example, some time ago we were working with a community water project in a rural area. The community members were not paying their minimal monthly financial contributions and this was jeopardizing the sustainability of the water supply. As we traveled to a number of villages, we asked people: "Why are you not paying for the water?" Many answered: "We are poor and do not have money." Others said: "The water should be free because the big development agency involved is very rich and can afford to meet all the costs with their 'financial muscle.'" Still others questioned: "We are not sure that the money we give would even be used for maintaining the water supply. It might be eaten."

We started by asking them: "Where were you getting water before the 'piped' water provided by the project?" They responded that there were other water sources, but these were unsanitary. We then asked: "What were the consequences of using those sources?" They said they got sick from diarrhea and dysentery and sometimes cholera. We asked them: "So where did you go for treatment?" They said that because there were rarely any medicines in free government hospitals, they were forced to go to private hospitals and clinics, which were more expensive. Before we finished asking them these questions they were already seeing the contradictions arising out of their non-payment. They were paying at the private hospitals or clinics many times more than what was demanded for the water project. We went further to ask them: "How would you feel if someone took over all your responsibility for your families and did everything for you? What would happen to your dignity? Would your self-respect be enhanced or diminished? What would your children and spouses think about you?" We also probed their fears about the financial mismanagement, asking them, "Has there been a case of financial abuse that you think might recur?" They answered, "No, nothing like that has ever happened." So we said they should perhaps ask themselves instead, "What if your money would not be abused?" This simple process of people realizing the inherent contradictions in their behavior led them to take responsibility for solving the development problem, and the monthly contributions increased dramatically.

At the national level, we are often left frustrated by our leaders refusing to address the clear contradictions, such as conspicuous consumption and corruption in government. Yet the profound example of Nelson Mandela emerging from 27 years of incarceration to preach forgiveness and unity prevented the widely predicted bloodbath from accompanying the transition from apartheid. The Truth and Reconciliation Commission that Mandela later set up to deal with the atrocities had no power to punish, only to listen and hear and grant amnesty. This difficult process was a very profound national example of confronting the excruciating contradiction of hearing the depths of inhumanity that people had descended to and being able to respond only with forgiveness, not revenge.

At the international level, there seem to be precious few examples of us really confronting our contradictions to move forward, though the Jubilee 2000 debt campaign stands out as an exception. International trading relations, so clearly replete with such contradictions, remain largely impervious to fundamental change. For example, for aid to resume to Malawi (the country where I come from), the International Monetary Fund (IMF) recently required Malawi to implement sweeping changes to the government support to poor farmers through privatizing the agriculture marketing board and reducing fertilizer subsidies. When asked about the double standards of U.S. subsidies for steel or EU subsidies for agriculture, the head of the IMF delegation mumbled: "Yes, we disagree with those too, but there is nothing we can do about those."

Refusing to face such contradictions prevents authentic international development.

A responsibility-based approach—The process of confronting contradictions

If I had not been in prison I would not have been able to achieve the most difficult task in life, and that is changing yourself.—Nelson Mandela

If you treat well the cat in your hands the one in the tree will come down of its own accord.

The essence of a turning point in development or change processes is when people confront their contradictions and take responsibility for the solutions themselves. It is when people begin to *judge each day not by its harvest but by the seeds they sow into it.* We cannot change the external situation before changing the internal situation. The internal situation is the only one we have some control over. Yet our tendency is to try to "conquer outer space while ignoring inner space."

Research among non-profit leaders (James, 2003) into their change processes as leaders highlighted the importance of internal change being at the center of external change. James found that leaders changed when they:

> ...were confronted with information that considerably challenged their preferred ways of leading, they entered a crucible experience. Like all of us, their instinctive reaction was denial and to externalize the blame. The respondents were able to move beyond blaming others and accepted responsibility for it. But even when they accepted responsibility for a problem, they had not arrived. They found themselves in an *'internal battle.'* This was not a pleasant place to be. It was a dark and confused place. Many of us prefer not to venture into our depths as we are frightened or ashamed of what we will find. If we dare enter our 'hearts of darkness,' we have to be courageous to resist the temptation to quickly flee. Change occurred in the respondents when they realized that who they thought they were and who they actually were, were two different people. There was a realization that what they believed about themselves and how they were behaving were not the same things. To a degree, this challenged their very identity.

This process of confronting contradictions is an essential element in development and all change processes. As George Santayana said: "Those who cannot remember the past are condemned to repeat it" (quoted by Tutu 1999). But it is often avoided because it is too painful to look inside, have our consciences awakened and accept the weight of responsibility for making change happen.

The face of change

A pioneer missionary noticed among the Masai he had been teaching, an old man named Keriko in obvious pain. He was certain the old man was ill. But his Masai catechist, Paul, chuckled at his concern. He said: "Are you worried about old man Keriko? Don't worry, he is all right. You see, for a Masai there is not much need to think in life. Almost everything he learns, he learns by memory or by rote...he learns about food, clothes, houses, cattle, grasses and women by memory...even things about God and religion. When he needs an answer to a question, all he has to do is to reach into his memory and come up with the correct answer. He can reach adulthood without thinking at all. What you are asking Keriko to do is to take the first thought about Masai brotherhood and the second thought of the human race and the God of all tribes and put these two thoughts together to make a new thought. This is a very difficult work. What you are witnessing in Keriko is the pain on the face of a man who is thinking for the first time in his life."
Source: Smith (2001: 250 – 1)

The "pain on the face of a man who is thinking" is someone confronting his contradictions. We rarely witness this pain in our development and change efforts. In fact, we try to avoid it. Instead, we see the increasingly tired and superficial smiles of people being promised that change will come—from the outside, from us, from the government. Development and change efforts fail when they do not challenge individuals, communities or organizations to make the link between their situations and their own decisions and actions (choices). It is only the pain of this link that catalyzes developmental motion. The more pain people experience, the more they will be willing to confront themselves and bring creative change.

The gaps in current development approaches

We recently visited an African village that boasted 15 projects implemented by 10 different non-profit organizations. There were projects dealing with HIV/AIDS; community school development; safe motherhood; breast-feeding; food security; environmental management; gender; human rights; children's rights; water supply; income-generating activities; radio-listening clubs; civic education; orphan care; and support for aged people. The different non-profits used a plethora of different development approaches and tools, including Participatory Rural Appraisal (PRA), Participatory Learning and Action (PLA), Training for Transformation, Appreciative Inquiry, Theatre for Development and "the 9-point method." Most non-profit bodies had their own committees and some individuals in the village belonged to as many as six different committees. The people in the village could have an average of three meetings per day with officers from the different organizations. Each of the organizations gave the people an allowance for attending a meeting—the breast-feeding committee was the most coveted because its organization gave the highest allowances even though there was no problem about breast-feeding in the village. Years of incessant development activity had brought no significant change. Most of the development approaches used did not take the confronting of contradiction seriously enough. By missing out on the painful change process, they also avoided mobilizing the necessary energy and passion for change. Looking at many of the popular approaches to development, such as participatory rural appraisal (PRA), appreciative inquiry, rights-based approaches and sector-wide approaches, we can see how in practice (though perhaps not in theory) this essential element of change is ignored.

PRA has undoubtedly revolutionized community development approaches by putting people, especially the vulnerable, at the center of planning processes. Yet PRA in practice often does not include the contradiction stage. A PRA process rarely asks: What type of people must we be to realize our vision? What prevents us from realizing our vision? What must we change in ourselves in order to realize our vision?

PRA tends to be "externally" rather than "externally and internally" focused. The process often tends to emphasize that the "oppressor" is out there in the environment. While this is usually true, a greater "oppressor" is often in the people themselves. Until the people have come to see this fact, they will keep externalizing and not owning their challenges.

In organizational capacity building, the appreciative inquiry (AI) approach has redressed the problem-oriented approach to change. It has demonstrated the need for a clear, inspiring and shared vision as the engine for development as well as for positive introspection as a means of self-discovery. AI has shown the importance of feeding an individual's or a group's strengths and starving the weaknesses, and focusing on solutions rather than problems.

But like PRA, AI does not address the contradiction stage, failing to ask the difficult questions related to contradictions in past behavior. An authentic development process demands that between "what is" and "what might be," people must explore their contradictions. But AI in practice tends to downplay the reasons that people are not yet in their "what might be" phase. AI tends not to provoke sufficient crisis and pain, which are the antidote for inertia and prerequisites for developmental motion. Trying to help people move toward their vision without addressing contradictions is like applying the accelerator while keeping your foot firmly on the brake pedal.

Rights-based approaches (RBA) theory acknowledges that responsibilities are the other side of the coin, but the emphasis is still on my rights. A few years ago my then six-year-old daughter came back from school excited by a new poem she had learned called "my rights." She recited perfectly:

Good education is my right
Good clothes are my right
Good food is my right
Privacy is my right

A name is my right
Medical care is my right
Unbiased information is my right
Choosing my friends is my right

I asked her if she had also learned another poem called "My responsibilities." She looked confused and said "No, Daddy."

In a similar vein, we were recently working with a women's rights non-profit organization, whose mission is to empower women to know, claim, and practice their rights (on such issues as property grabbing by a man's relatives when the husband dies). In our work, we observed in one family in which both married sons had died, but property was only grabbed from one of the daughters-in-law. When we asked why, they said that one of the daughters-in-law had "become one of them" through the way she had nurtured good relations with the extended family, so how could they take property from "one of their own"?

> *In relationships one cannot do evil but to oneself and one cannot do good but to oneself.*

When we mentioned this to our clients at the non-profit organization, they were not pleased. They felt that women had no responsibility for addressing the problem themselves, and that by trying to show women contradictions in their behavior that might exacerbate property grabbing, this would take them away from their mandate of "purely teaching the women to know, claim and practice their rights." They felt this was all that was necessary for development to occur.

Similarly on a national level, the Poverty Reduction Strategy Paper (PRSP) processes moves people toward agreed poverty reduction outcomes based on the analysis of causes of poverty and the strategy design. The need for the country to go through a contradiction process is rarely mentioned.

All of these approaches to development at different levels have in common the notion that development external activity is the way of moving from the current situation to a desired situation.[1] This can be illustrated by the common development model below:

---

[1] This is a description of how PRA, AI, and PRSPs are practiced in Malawi and many other places. In some cases, good practitioners are able to help people face their contradictions using these methods. But this is not a specific goal of these approaches.

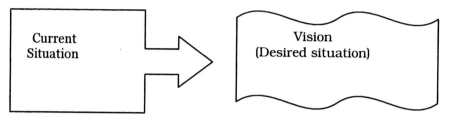

In reality, development processes encounter a wall of contradiction as illustrated in a simplified linear way below:

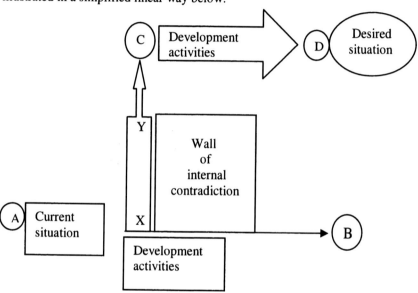

Development activities on AB cannot make people realize their vision (desired situation). Development activities can only help people to realize their vision if it is being implemented on CD. For people to work at the CD level, they must overcome the wall of internal contradictions by moving up the XY line. This is the conscious action of *judging each day not by its harvest but by the seed we sow into it.*

The more we begin to see the demands that development makes on us, the more we will begin to understand that the "being" must precede the "doing." Development efforts must therefore focus on both. If the "being" does not change, it can only reproduce the "doing" of today and no more. It is incapable of doing differently. Any attempt to improve the doing without changing the being will only result in failure at worst and unsustainable improvements at best. People cannot get to a higher level without understanding how they were responsible for the lower level they are today.

Implementing a responsibility-based approach in practice

We have shown that the missing element in most development processes is the contradiction stage—the failure to *judge each day not by its harvest but by the seed we sow into it.* We have also shown that most development efforts concentrate on and emphasize how to help people get out of their undesired situations. They do not attach the same importance on why people are in their undesired situations. The emphasis is on external factors and not the human (*responsibility*) factors creating and maintaining the status quo. Development is the awakening of consciousness—the consciousness of one's obligations and responsibilities. This is our main task in development.

But exactly how do we do this? How do we help people see the contradictions in their lives? How do we help them to *judge each day not by its harvest but by the seeds they sow into it?* How do we help people to confront their shadows so that they can liberate themselves on their paths of development?

A responsibility-based approach involves faith, relationship, heartfelt vision, confronting contradiction, strategizing, and implementing. A brief description of each follows.

Faith. Saying that the poor are responsible for their own development makes intellectual sense. But seeing the realities of people and their problems, such a point of view is an act of "faith." As development practitioners, we need to honestly ask ourselves whether we really believe that the people we are working with can fundamentally change. If we have lost this faith and become cynical through disillusioning experiences, it is better to leave the development field. Sadly, too many employees of the "development industry" do not really believe that the people they are trying to help *can* change. They are reluctant to give responsibility to the people they work with because they consider it to be too risky for "purposes of accountability." It is important to see that the risk involved in allowing the freedom of decision making is that [people] may be left floundering, unsure how to proceed, prone to making hasty decisions. The best way to offset this risk is not to prescribe rules and impose decisions, but to encourage reflection and critical discussion, and to make sure that appropriate guidance is available when the [people] seek it. This is the way to help the people to develop their capacity to govern themselves.

Relationship. A development practitioner must establish a relationship of mutual respect and trust with the people he or she is trying to help. Development occurs best within a relationship characterized by warmth, trust, and mutual respect. The goal is for the development practitioner and the people he or she is trying to help to become comfortable with each other. This may mean staying in an area for some time and building rapport with the people before starting any "visible" projects.

> *It is better to be surrounded by people than to be surrounded by things.*

Attending weddings, funerals, traditional court cases, visiting people in their homes, attending communal events, visiting people in the gardens and learning the local language are some of the ways to achieve this. These activities not only help the practitioner to create relationships of trust with the people, but also help him or her to better understand the people. Understanding the people's mindset is key to unlocking their potential.

Heartfelt vision. In the early 2000s many developing countries developed their "Vision 2020"—an ideal picture of what a country should be by the year 2020. Today, in most of these countries, almost no one remembers what that vision was, and no one is talking about it. What has gone wrong?

We believe that a vision must engage people's emotions if it is to be motivating. During a nationwide consultation on people's experiences, feelings, and aspirations in 2002, we were surprised to find how many people and communities could not articulate their desired futures. The general attitude was that things have always been bad.

> *What the eyes have seen, the heart cannot forget*

They are now getting worse, so how can we logically hope for a better future? My colleague related a story in one community about how, when he was a child in a family of eight children, they all used to go to visit their grandparents in their village. He said they would sometimes stay for three months at the grandparents' home, and they did not need to bring anything from town because the grandparents were self-sufficient. He said that today, if he wants to go and see his parents in the rural home with his four children, he has to bring all of the supplies with him from town, otherwise they will starve. The reaction to the story was telling; the young people in the group laughed and thought he was joking, because they had not seen a grandparent who could host 10 visitors from town for three months without needing their support. The elder members agreed and but looked very concerned. They asked, "What has gone wrong with us, where did we miss it?"

Developing a genuine and authentic vision with people who have lost hope requires us to engage people's emotions. If people are without hope, then rational, intellectual planning is meaningless. Nothing will change, no matter what plans are put in place. As a result, we try to touch people's emotions in facilitating any development work. We ask questions like: "What type of country or what type of life do you want your children to have when they grow up?" We need to see our desired futures with our hearts.

Such a vision-crafting process kindles a fire in the community. It creates motivation and enthusiasm. People start feeling pulled to their desired future. Their next natural questions are "When shall we get there?" or "How shall we arrive there?" We must avoid the temptation to jump into strategizing or to leapfrog the crucial contradiction stage, where people are challenged to confront their shadows.

Confronting contradiction. An effective development process combines a vivid inspiring picture of where you want to go with a hard, convicting understanding of where you are now and why. It is this gap that is the source of pain and motivation for developmental motion. A development practitioner must find a way to intensify the brilliance of both the vision and the current reality as a way of maintaining the pain and motivation.

The climax of the contradiction stage is when people see that the future is not arrived at accidentally, but is created through our decisions and actions—our choices. People need to understand that just as the future is created through choices, the present was also created by the decisions and actions of yesterday. A development practitioner may need to challenge people to seriously reflect on how their choices yesterday have created the current undesired situation. People need to ask themselves: "What have I been doing or not doing that has contributed to the current undesired situation?" Honest introspection can lead to healthy surfacing of contradictions and a clear understanding of what needs to be changed in ourselves. Now people are taking responsibility for change.

We need to ask developmental questions that reveal to people why they have not got the results they want. And we must show them that getting the results is largely within their "circle of influence"—and therefore their responsibility. We are not asking ourselves the right questions, and we might do well to learn from the example below.

When people have undergone a contradiction, they are more determined to own and be involved in the creation of their desired future. It is only then that such concepts as participation and involvement become meaningful. People must be convinced that, *"Do not ask God to protect you and then do things that harm you"* and that *"many people smear themselves with mud and then complain that they are dirty."* The next stage, therefore, is for the development practitioner to support the people and constantly keep them focused on the vision while further challenging them to recognize and deal with further contradictions along the way.

Strategizing and implementing. The next challenge is how to maintain momentum and motivation and how to help people not to revert to former ways. People need rewards and incentives to change. The development practitioner must help people to recognize and celebrate their successes, no matter how small. He or she must help them to see how their taking responsibility is paying off. The development practitioner must also help them to understand that setbacks are normal and that they are part of the process.

In practical terms, it is important to create time for reflection and learning. The reflection and learning sessions must focus on achievements and failures of the initiatives and linking of these to taking responsibility and making choices. The learning sessions should show how the people's choices led to the achievements and failures. The more people see these links, the more they will believe that they, indeed, have created their own destinies.

The action point of such reflections is to encourage people to take more responsibility to achieve more and address their challenges. The development practitioner must always maintain an attitude of support and challenge along the process. The results of each reflection and learning session must be documented, and each subsequent session must be built on the previous ones. This helps to build increasing consciousness along the process. It helps the people to see how the journey is progressing. Monitoring and evaluation systems and management information systems and procedures therefore must include the "consciousness raising" component. They must generate data that will be used to demonstrate how taking or abdicating responsibility will affect the progress of the project and therefore the attainment of, or the failure to attain, the vision.

Conclusions on responsibility-based development

If you really want to go to Mount Olympus, make sure every step you make takes you nearer there—Socrates
We keep learning from bitter experience that we cannot change other people. Personal development is a personal responsibility. Organizational development is the organization's responsibility, and similarly, national development is a national responsibility. All development is self-development. No person can develop another and no country can develop another. They can only assist or hinder the development of the other. *The sympathizer cannot mourn more than the bereaved.* As development practitioners, all we can do is create the conditions for people to become aware of their contradictions and encourage them to respond. This is not a very easy approach to sell to donors, clients, or even our own egos. It means that we give up our vain attempts to command other people, communities, and nations to develop and control them. This leaves us with the pain of having to stand by when people refuse to confront their contradictions and change. In his closing speech at the 2004 International HIV/AIDS conference in Thailand, Nelson Mandela said, "We know what we should do, what is missing is the *will* to do it." In other words, we want a good harvest without sowing the right seed.

We cannot dictate other people's choices, however tempting that may be. We cannot force people to confront their contradictions. But we can create the conditions and situations where this is more likely to happen. We need to design it into our change processes, rather than hope it happens by accident.

This chapter has shown that awakening the consciousness of individuals, families, communities, organizations, and nations toward their responsibility and obligation for their own development through contradiction and self-confrontation processes is the way toward truly sustainable development. It is much more than | *The river that forgets its source will soon dry up.* |
simply planning, monitoring, and evaluating new activities. We need to focus on how people need to "*be*" to make the initiatives more effective and sustainable. Ultimately, people's "*doing*" cannot rise above their "*being.*" Similarly, the doing of the development worker or the change agent cannot rise above his or her being, as is emphasized by the saying, *Who you are speaks so loud I can't hear what you are doing.*

Just as the slave trade came to an end when people confronted their shadows; colonization came to an end when people confronted their shadows;

one-party states and life presidencies came to an end when people confronted their shadows; apartheid in South Africa came to an end when people confronted their shadows, so the global, continental, national, and societal challenges we are facing today will only be addressed when we have the courage to confront our contradictions. *Many people smear themselves with mud and then complain that they are dirty.* Unless people realize that they are dirty because they smeared themselves with mud, they will not change. People must be helped to realize that *if they climb a tree they must climb down the same tree.* This is the essence of contradiction and responsibility-based development.

Conclusion on spirituality and work

Service is a central feature of spirituality. The benefits of spirituality ensue from service. For Victor Frankl, spirituality is in essence self-transcendence and human freedom. The freedom also implies obligation—responsibility for something or to someone. It is the use of this freedom to act responsibly that uncovers the meaning of our lives. It is the exercise of spiritual freedom and responsibility that produces such effects as peace of mind, good conscience, and contentment. These are byproducts of the exercise of spiritual freedom and responsibility. It is not possible to pursue them directly. They ensue naturally for the individual who lives for something else or Someone greater (Covey, 2004: 315 – 316). In every soul there has been deposited the seed of a great future, but that seed will never germinate, much less grow to maturity, except through the rendering of useful service (Hill, 1966: 105).

Spirituality, like real power, is not private property. It only becomes useful when used. It must flow from the person to touch others through work. Spirituality is transcendent. It is always about touching others. The spiritual attention to work is further emphasized by the late Steve Jobs when he said:

> Your work is going to fill a large part of your life, and the only way to be truly satisfied is to do what you believe is great work. And the only way to do great work is to love what you do. If you haven't found it keep looking, don't settle. As with all matters of the heart, you will know when you find it. And like any great relationship, it gets better and better as the years roll on. So keep looking until you find it. Don't settle (Steve Jobs, 2005 Quoted in *Nation on Sunday*, October 9, 2011).

A key challenge for change efforts is that they do not go deep enough to effect fundamental change. They do not go deep enough to enable people to identify, surface, and confront their contradictions and shadows. A key explanation for this is a lack of spiritual insight as a key ingredient for the change efforts.

CHAPTER 3: UNDERSTANDING THE HUMAN SPIRIT

Introduction

Spirituality is being aware or conscious of one's physical and spiritual environments for personal balance and effectiveness. It is the basis of personal power. It is the ability to be present, notice, make meaning, and interpret one's physical and spiritual environments. While spirituality is an end in itself, it must necessarily add value to all aspects of one's life, including effectiveness in one's work. If spirituality does not add value, then it is not a worthwhile pursuit. A spiritual student must be a better student, a spiritual farmer must be a better farmer, a spiritual lawyer must be a better lawyer, a spiritual doctor must be a better doctor, a spiritual engineer must be a better engineer; and a spiritual development worker must be a better development worker. A very spiritual but incompetent individual is an anomaly. A spiritual person is competent because he or she knows where they can make the most difference or contribution and concentrates his or her energy there. This however should not be misunderstood to mean that all competent people are spiritual.

Life is one indivisible whole. Just as we cannot divide or separate the biological and the psychological, we cannot separate the spiritual. I remember at the very beginning of my work life asking God when I would start serving Him. I did not think the "secular" work I was doing was His work. I remember hearing in my heart, "You are serving me right where you are and in what you are doing." Spirituality takes a holistic view to life. It is not about the non-physical, non-material, and non-bodily aspects of life only. It is an integration of all aspects of life body, mind, and spirit. In relative terms, there is material poverty in the developing nations and there is spiritual poverty in the developed nations. Both are unnatural human conditions. The natural human condition is freedom of the body, the mind, and the spirit. True spirituality aims at the health of the body, mind and spirit. It aims at wholeness.

A clarification of some key terms used in the book is given below:

Faith—what one believes in
Spirituality—how we relate to the supernatural to give meaning and a basis for reflection, decision, and action
Religion—an institutionalized set of beliefs and practices regarding the spiritual realm

Source: James (2011).

The body, the mind and the spirit

The conventional concept of a human being is dualistic. A person is seen as comprising the body and the mind. The body is the visible corporal part, while the mind is the invisible part. While there is truth in this conceptualization, from a deeper understanding, this conceptualization is limited. For a fuller and deeper understanding, a human being is looked at as a tripartite entity comprising the body, the mind, and the spirit (Nee, 1977: 21; 1965: 5). The spirit is that which psychologists call the *subconscious*. I prefer to call it spirit because *spirit* carries more meaning for me. Whether one calls it spirit or subconscious mind does not matter; what matters is what its functions are and what roles and functions it plays.

Through the body the person comes into contact with the material world. The body gives the person his or her world consciousness. The mind reveals his or her personality and gives the person his or her self-consciousness. Through the spirit, one comes into contact with the spiritual world and therefore the spirit gives the person his or her spiritual consciousness. The body is the container of the mind and the mind is the container of the spirit.

The body is the seat of the five senses: sight, smell, hearing, touch, and taste. A healthy body is important for spirituality as *health is wealth.* As true wealth always have a spiritual dimension.

The mind is the seat of the will, the intellect and the emotions. The will, the intellect, and the emotions are what constitute an individual's personality.

The intellect consists of thoughts, concepts, ideas, philosophies, and memories, among others. They are there in a rather fixed way. They do not change by themselves. They are called mindsets.

The emotions consist of emotional feelings, experiences, and sympathies, among others. These form fixed attitudes and prejudices.

The will consists of conditioned skills and reflexes, one's abilities and drives and defense mechanisms, among others. These are built up through past training, and are described as habits. The will is the seat of the *I* in the person.

The spirit or the subconscious mind is the seat of the intuition, communion, and conscience. Just as the body is a tool for getting information from the physical environment through the five senses, the spirit is a tool for getting information from the spiritual or the supernatural environment. The conscience is the seat of one's values: the sense of what is right or wrong; or what is important and not important to the individual. The intuition is the way of accessing "supernatural wisdom" (knowing without direct learning and guidance through the still small voice).

Communion is a way of linking up to the spiritual world or transcendence, which makes accessing the "supernatural wisdom" and guidance possible. Simply, it is the capacity for prayer.

Robert Collier calls the discovery of the subconscious or the spirit the greatest discovery of all time as far as self-development is concerned. It is the discovery that man has within himself the power to control his surroundings—that one is not at the mercy of luck or chance—that one is the creator of one's own destiny. Man is the master of the creative force working in him. Joseph Murphy (1988: 2) calls the human spirit the secret of the ages. Napoleon Hill believed that the human spirit is the "sixth sense," which is the creative part of our minds, regulating our intuition and creating our hunches and inspiration (Vernon, 2007: 81).

The spirit is the noblest, highest, deepest, and most powerful part of the human being. If comparisons were to be made, one would say that the body has arithmetic power. The mind has geometric power, while the spirit has exponential power. All genuine miracles that stagger and outstrip human understanding are wrought through the power of the spirit.

The spirit is also the basis of all great leadership. There is no great leader who does not draw from the power of the spirit. The spiritual realm is the most powerful—and at the same time, the least understood—evidenced by the fact that most people do not know that they have a spirit, or they do not feel or cannot locate where their spirit is. This explains, in part, why great leaders are always a rare commodity.

In all self-development efforts, the spirit is the least understood and the most neglected component. Peter Drucker, the eminent management guru, emphasized this point when he said, "The individual needs the return to spiritual values, for he can survive in the present human situation only by affirming that man is not just a biological and psychological being but also a spiritual being, that is creature, and existing for the purpose of his creator and subject to Him."

He went on to emphasize that people can only find meaning in faith and not in work. In my opinion, this understanding is one of the key factors that set Peter Drucker apart from a myriad of his contemporaries. His ability to draw from the spirit could be what gave his writings a never-ending freshness that is difficult to explain otherwise.

In the individual consciously practicing self-development, the spirit plays the role of governance; the mind plays the role of management while the body plays the role of operations. The body is the container of the mind. The mind is the container of the spirit. Effective self-development is possible when all the three components: the spirit, the mind, and the body are undertaking their appropriate roles. When one or two are not, effectiveness is hampered.

Because we largely live in a world of the five senses and the mind, most effort in self-development is applied to body and mind development. Physical education is mostly directed at the body, while professional education is generally directed at the intellect. The spirit is not consciously targeted among most individuals. Indeed, spiritual development is a dark area, as evidenced by the fact that the average person does not know they have a spirit and they cannot locate it within themselves.

The body is developed through appropriate nutrition, exercise, and sufficient rest. The mind is developed through constructive information and disciplining the will, and by governing one's emotions. The mind is the meeting point of the spirit and the body. By the spirit a person communicates with the spiritual world, and through the body via the five senses a person communicates with the natural or physical environment. The mind stands between the natural and the spiritual and belongs to both. Since the mind contains the power of the independent will, it decides (or it can be trained) to choose whether to follow the spirit or the body on what issues and at what time. The mind, therefore, is the seat of personality and it is the self.

Spirituality does not separate the body, the mind and the spirit as the following proverbs show: *the body is the mouth piece of the spirit, strength of the mind strengthens the body;* and *when the body and the spirit match, one becomes a saint.*

The body

If we understand spirituality to mean the ability to be present, notice, make meaning, and interpret, it implies the ability to use the body (the five senses) as a tool for learning. The key senses for learning are listening and observation (seeing).

Listening

How well do we listen when someone is talking to us? Listening is not the same as hearing. Hearing does not require any energy, but listening does. Listening is intentional, and therefore requires an investment of energy. There is nothing more energy-draining as real listening. I sometimes spend eight hours a day conducting individual coaching sessions of one hour each. At the end of the day I am so tired I cannot do anything else. However, one observes two types of individuals in such sessions: those who are stuck in their personal development, and those who seem to be making progress. Those who are stuck seem to suck energy out of you. Those who are making progress seem to be bouncing their positive energy on you, reinvigorating you in the process. Developmental coaching is an area in which listening skills become very critical for success.

Effective listening goes beyond listening to what one is saying. If a wife is in one room and calls to her husband who is watching TV in another room, asking him if he hears the baby who is crying in the bedroom, she is usually asking more than her words are saying. If the husband is not sensitive, he will answer "Yes" or "No" and keep on watching TV. If he is sensitive, he will understand the question. He may not even need to answer with words. He will simply stop watching TV and walk to the bedroom to attend to the baby. This is what is called active listening.

Effective or active listening must happen at three levels. One needs to listen to the words being said. If you don't get the content, chances are you will give a wrong response. It is like giving a right answer to a wrong question on an exam. How many times do people give completely wrong answers because they make wrong assumptions of the context of the question? When parents or adults are talking about their friends or some other people, children—especially at the kindergarten level—will usually chip in and ask, "Oh, do you mean the Mary, who is my classmate?" To them, that's the Mary they know and if somebody is talking about Mary, she must be the one. This underscores the importance of understanding content and its context. This requires paying attention and spending energy.

The second level of listening is listening to the feelings of the person. As they are talking, how are they feeling? Are they happy? Are they sad? Are they confused? Are they worried? Are they afraid? When one listens to the feelings in the content or feelings in the context and how they are being expressed, they can identify what the speaker is feeling. This enables one to empathize with the speaker.

Beyond the feelings, one needs to listen to the intent of the speaker. What does he or she want? Like the husband watching TV, the content of the question is clear. He can answer "Yes" or "No." However, if he does this, he has answered at the content level, which will only infuriate his wife because he has not answered to her feelings. She is uncomfortable and unhappy that the child is crying. But again, it is not enough to empathize with her. He must listen at the intent level—what does she want him to do? He must respond not by words but by action. He must go to the bedroom and attend to the baby.

Talking and listening go together. Talking is related to saying the right word to the right person at the right time. Many people have been injured by words. Spouses have destroyed each other's self-esteem through careless words. Parents have destroyed their children's self-esteem and confidence through negative and destructive words.

Effective speaking usually flows from effective listening. Effective listening, real listening or active listening will give one the most effective words for the moment. The rule is always to speak less and listen more. *The person who talks incessantly talks nonsense* and God *gave us two ears and one mouth so that we can listen as twice as we talk.* In developmental coaching, we are taught to listen 70 percent and talk 30 percent. *There is more wisdom in listening than in talking.* In practice, however this is hard to do because we often feel that we have so much to say. It requires a lot of discipline to suppress your words. It also requires faith that the other person knows what is best for them, that they know what they want, and that their choice is the best for them. It requires humility to suppress our own intelligence and trust in theirs.

The best words one can give in such situations come in the form of questions. As they process the questions they clarify their own thinking. Intervention becomes necessary only when they are stuck. Only human beings can speak, and this is one attribute that makes them nearest to God. Through words, they can create for good or for evil. The ability to use words to create for good is a key requirement in spiritual development. *Quarrels may end but words once spoken never die.* Appropriate use of words is a key skill in helping people. *A cutting word is worse than a bow string,* and *a cut may heal but the cut of the tongue does not.*

By listening to a person, you begin to know them—you get to know their personality. A person's words will reveal his or her goals, values, frustrations, and many other things. This will give a clue as to the rights words to use.

Observation
I read a poem, author anonymous:

> There was an old owl who sat on a branch of an old tree
> He sat and watched
> The less he spoke, the more he saw
> The more he saw, the less he spoke
> Therefore he decided to speak less in order to see more

Observation is a key skill in learning. People never say everything you need to know. We always censor our words in our own interest. Also, people may not answer our questions to the level of detail we want. A key skill in communication is the ability to hear what the other person is *not* saying. This is only possible through keen observation skills. It also takes skill to observe correctly, especially when operating in a different context—"never assume" is always a safe caution. It is in observation that the principle of being present, noticing, making meaning and interpretation is most important. When I went to Juba, Southern Sudan a few years ago, I was surprised to find the latest state-of-the-art cars in numbers I had not seen in many African cities. I also observed that while the people had very expensive cars, most of them did not have proper housing. Many houses had no electricity or running water. I wondered about the people's priorities until I understood that because they had been living through a war that had lasted 22 years, it did not make sense to invest in a house, which could be bombed or torched at any time. Investing in a car made sense—a car allows you to be mobile or even to run away.

The mind

Buckminster Fuller (1969: 290 – 291) observed that "man has found that he is endowed with a powerful brain, which has found out what a few of the invisible principles operative in the physical universe can do. But the universe, having permitted him to discover his intellectual effectiveness as well as some of the universe's riches, and thus to participate consciously as well as subconsciously in universal evolution, will now require him to use his intellect directly and effectively. Success and failure is now all of humanity's responsibility."

Three elements constitute the mind. These are the will, the intellect, and the emotions.

The will

The will is the self. It is the I. It is the person. It is the decision-making faculty. It is the will that makes man a free moral or sovereign agent or entity—through his ability to choose what he wants. No power in the universe can usurp this sovereignty. Man must give his consent before giving away this sovereignty or he may give it away through ignorance. Man is free at the moment he decides to be. It is the will that gives a person his or her individuality. It is also through the will that one decides to relate with the Spirit or not. Such a relationship can only be personal and may not be delegated because, *God has no grand children.*

It is through the will that an individual may determine his or her purpose or mission in life and to this one may align all of one's major decisions in life. One is only powerful when they are acting within their purpose or mission, *a rooster cannot crow in a foreign land.*

It is through this sense of mission or purpose that people can project a trajectory of their lives and decide what personal wars and battles to be involved in. The war is the overall strategy driving people toward their identified life goal—what does one want to achieve by the end of one's life? Battles are the strategic issues one deals with in the course of one's life. *In the great river of life there are large and small fish.* The conscious person chooses his or her battles carefully, and only chooses those battles that will contribute to the overall goal. One's focus is on the overall goal. Whether or not one wins the battles, one must be conscious enough to use the results to move and contribute toward the overall goal. *Life is a gift but beautiful living is a gift of wisdom.*

I remember working with members of civil society organizations who were engaging with what they considered a recalcitrant government in a frustrating dialogue process. I asked them whether they were able to differentiate between the battle and the war they were fighting. The war was to ensure that the government did not win again in the next elections if it did not change by aligning itself to the needs and interests of the citizens. The elections were coming within the next 30 months. The dialogue process was just one of the battles. If they got their demands met, it would strengthen their position and legitimacy in the eyes of the citizens. They could use their appeal to significantly influence the citizens to vote the government out if it had not changed. If the government did not meet their demands, they would use that result to show the citizens how uncaring the government was. In a way, it did not matter whether the demands were met or not. They could use either result in achieving their overall goal. A loss would even be a better option, as the government's perceived alienation from the people would do more damage to its goal of being re-elected.

Helping others in their personal development processes is often much more difficult than we imagine. This truth became more clear to me one day when my daughter who was at that time eight years old came to me and said, "Dad I am not happy being between number 12 to 15 in class every time I write tests and exams. I want you to teach me how to be number one." Believing that *to teach is to learn twice,* I gladly accepted her request. She was excited and I thought it was easy.

In the first week we met everyday in the evenings going through her day's work at school and her homework. But by the end of the first week it was already clear that I was not going to succeed. The subject matter they were learning was largely unfamiliar to me. It is many years ago when I was in primary school and couldn't remember much of the material. In many instances the curriculum has changed beyond recognition. When I made some comments and suggestions, she kept reminding me, "Dad, the teacher did not say so." In addition, by the nature of my work, I could not always be at home every evening.

I then realized that I am not a (primary school teacher) and I could not competently intervene at content level. I needed to put in place a support mechanism that would compensate for my lack of competence in content and my continuous absences from home. I talked with my wife and we designed a four step plan for her:

1. To plant in the daughter the belief and self confidence that she is intelligent. We told her that every evening when praying before going to sleep she should thank God for creating her an intelligent girl and tell God that she is going to show her gratitude by working extra hard in her school work.

2. I worked with her to develop a sense of mission—to already see herself in the secondary school of her admiration and believe that the eventual fulfillment of the vision is inevitable.

3. Together with her, I assessed her performance reports and identified the subjects in which her performance was weak and we hired the best teacher we could afford to give her extra tuition from the basics in a way that made learning a pleasure and fun.

4. I undertook to motivate, support and challenge her through thanking her for any little progress we noted, showing more interest in her home work; and sensitively challenging her whenever we observed some complacency.

The key lesson I learned from the whole process was *what you help a child to love is more important than what you help the child to learn.*

Some individuals are strong willed while others are weak willed. Whether individuals are born so is a question of debate, but it is clear that the will can be trained to become strong. Strong-willed people are determined people. They have the tenacity to hold on until they reach their ultimate goal. Strong-willed people do not accept the world as they found it. They shape it in their own image. Strong-willed people are optimistic and generally achieve more than weak-willed people. The down side of being strong willed is that they are likely to meet more frustrations in life, especially if they cannot differentiate between which battles are worth fighting.

Regarding the will, a few points need emphasis:

*   Ambition to be great is good and healthy.
*   Greatness requires great sacrifice.
*   Greatness requires determination—a whatever-it-may-take attitude. People who are strong willed are the ones who will make it in this life. Weak-willed people do not go very far.
*   How great one ultimately becomes has two sides—the human side and the "grace" side. Humanly, one must be ambitious, strong willed and make great sacrifices. It is grace, however, that will ultimately confer greatness on an individual. The greatest people are not necessarily the most ambitious, determined, or those who have sacrificed more than others. But there is justice in the universe. Those who try the most are the ones who generally make it.
*   Greatness on its own is neutral. It is the motive behind the ambition that makes it good or bad. Greatness whose motive is to exercise dominion and authority over others is bad greatness. It destroys both the people and the person holding it. It is not greatness in the true sense of the word. It makes the person a destructive force. Greatness whose primary purpose or motive is to serve people or humanity is good and real greatness. It builds people and the person holding it. Such individuals are builders of humanity, and they leave the world a better place than they found it.

The will is also the battlefield between good and evil. Both good and evil need human agency and consent. If one decides for good, good will prevail. If one decides for evil, evil will prevail. From this understanding, man plays a key role in determining the destiny of the world.

It is one's decisions and not one's conditions that determine one's destiny. Anthony Robbins (1997) emphasizes, "The human spirit is truly unconquerable. But the will to win, the will to succeed, to shape one's life, to take control, can only be harnessed when you decide what you want, and believe that no challenge, no problem, no obstacle can keep you from it. When you decide that your life will ultimately be shaped not by conditions, but by your decisions, then in a moment, your life will change forever."

Using the will to create the future we want is everybody's responsibility, especially the young people because they have longer futures than the older people. If you are a teacher don't think only about being a good teacher, think about how to change or transform the teaching profession so that it can in turn create more innovative people who can transform their countries, continents, and the whole world. If you are an engineer, do not think about only being a good engineer, but think about ways to transform the engineering profession to enable it to transform the country's or continent's technological and economic standing in the world. If you are a clergy person, do not think only about being a good ordinary pastor. Think about how you can use the pulpit to challenge people to wake up from their slumber to their different spiritual and developmental responsibilities. If you are a politician, do not only think about yourself and your constituency. Challenge yourself to think about how to transform the practice of politics, which has generally fallen into disrepute all over the world.

The future we aspire to is our responsibility. If we do not take this responsibility, then perhaps we should stop having children—otherwise what type of future are we throwing them into? We must be selfless enough to think not only about ourselves but also about our children and their children. This is our responsibility of stewardship.

The intellect

The intellect is the thinking faculty of the mind. It is upon this thinking that the will makes decisions and decides its allegiances. The will without a strong intellect is greatly incapacitated. It's like the baby who could not be consoled because his father could not take the moon from the sky to give him as a toy, and the other one who wanted her mother to take some cartoons from inside the TV screen because she liked them so much and therefore she wanted to add them to her teddy bears. The babies had a very strong will but not much intellect. They couldn't understand that what they were asking for was impossible. Development of the intellect is the major preoccupation of academic learning.

The intellect uses the information it gets for its thinking function. Thinking is a highly politicized issue. Thinking one's own thoughts is not always easy. Given the general concerns about the decline in moral and spiritual values, thinking is a major issue. How do you ensure that you are thinking your own thoughts and that you are thinking well? There is a lot of "group think" driven by the media. The media, especially TV, tells people what is fashionable. It teaches youths what modern values are. It is for this reason that TV, and also the Internet, are called "the third parent." In some houses, TV and the Internet have taken over the parenting role. Children learn about life and the world primarily from TV and not from their parents.

In modern society it takes a lot of courage for an individual to think one's own thoughts. When people decide to think their own thoughts, they are usually breaking away from the crowd and they may be isolated. Independent thinking is always dangerous to those who want to control others for their own self-interest. This is because the mind that can truly think cannot not be bought or corrupted.

It takes courage to rise above narrow and prejudiced thinking to begin seeing people primarily as individuals and human beings without classifying them. We still see some leaders in our continent who seem not to have evolved in their thinking to suit the requirements of modern leadership. They are still stuck in tribalism, nepotism, and tokenism.

One of the biggest challenges in our increasingly complex world is to cultivate independent and unbiased thinking that embraces diversity and that recognizes and supports good and rejects evil. Evil prevails when people are deprived of their freedom to think their own thoughts. It is appropriate thinking that encourages integrity—the ability to align one's decisions and actions to one's overall goal in life. A young man asked Socrates for the direction to Mount Olympus. Socrates did not tell the young man the direction to Mount Olympus. Instead he simply told him, "If you really want to go to Mount Olympus make sure every step you make takes you nearer there." A thinking person is consciously preoccupied with the questions—what is the Mount Olympus of my life or what is the ultimate goal of my life? How will the decisions I make and the actions I take help or hinder me from getting to my Mount Olympus? And how can I achieve more alignment in my life?

The future of a society is dependent on the type and level of thinking prevalent in that society. Margaret Wheatley in her forthcoming book, *So far from Home*, rightly observes: "We are rapidly losing the ability to think long and hard about anything, even those issues and topics we care about." Development efforts will be more effective if they concentrate more on promoting better thinking. Because of inappropriate thinking, some people no longer recognize what is right and what is wrong on what are otherwise very clear issues. I saw a letter to the editor in which a woman was asking whether it was right for her 23-year-old daughter to parade naked from the bathroom to her bedroom via the seating room in the presence of the mother and a 14-year-old brother.

In some African societies it has come to be silently accepted that there is nothing abnormal about a man cheating on his wife, but it is absolutely unacceptable for a wife to cheat on her husband. The same thinking also extends to allowing a man to marry more wives but never for a woman to marry more than one husband. It is right thinking that will enable society and individuals to surface and confront these contradictions.

Emotions

Emotions are an important support system to the intellect and the will. Positive emotions are an encouragement to the intellect and the will. Negative emotions are usually a caution. The faculty of emotions is the seat of what is referred to as emotional intelligence. The development of the intellect gives a person intellectual intelligence. The development of the emotions gives a person emotional intelligence. A proper use of the emotions provides information that a person can use in dealing with people and themselves more effectively. In order to do this, one must be able to:

Perceive emotions—this refers to the ability to empathize with others or to stand in their shoes emotionally. *See with others' eyes and they will see with yours.* This implies the ability to detect and interpret emotions by looking at people's faces, looking into their eyes (as it is said that the eyes are the window to the soul), looking at their pictures and cultural artifacts, and listening to their voices. This is the ability a woman uses to differentiate the cries of a baby, for example. She is able to differentiate between a cry of hunger, a cry just seeking attention, a cry of discomfort, and a cry that signifies danger.

This ability also signifies the ability to identify and feel one's own emotions. There are some people who are blocked from their own feelings and emotions.

Use emotions—this means the ability to use the emotions to contribute to the thinking process. Positive emotions are usually an encouragement, while negative emotions are usually a caution, but this usually has to be endorsed by the conscience.

Understand emotions—this means the ability to make meaning of what one is feeling or observing in others and interpret it into action. If I am feeling inferior in the presence of others, for example, the feeling may be telling me that I need to do more work on confidence building. If you are feeling afraid to tell your boss that you are unhappy with her unreasonable demands, the feeling may be telling you to do more work on your assertiveness.

A mixture of feelings may be telling one of the complexity of the situation one is dealing with and therefore the need for a more comprehensive action or response as compared to a simplistic one. There are times, for example, when one feels both excited and apprehensive about a prospect. This may mean that you need to seize the opportunity but you should also identify and deal with the aspects causing the fear or apprehension.

Manage emotions—to a conscious person, emotions are servants, not masters. They are messengers on one's journey of life. Both positive and negative emotions are saying something. When listened to, they will contribute positively to one's life purpose or to the situation at hand. Managing emotions means taking the action required by the emotion and letting the emotions be regulated by the conscience and the intellect. Just because it feels good does not always mean that it is right. Just because it does not feel good may not mean it is wrong. It is possible to have a very sweet poison and a very bitter medicine.

An example is the advice we give to children who have lost their appetite due to a fever: "Use your will and not your feelings to eat the food." It is also the basis of the statement: "Feel the fear and do it anyway."

Effective management of emotions is a key indicator of maturity in an individual. Failure to understand and manage emotions is a challenge among many, especially young couples. Many couples fail to understand that feelings of love do and must change over time, and that this is normal and natural. The intensity of feelings of love when one falls in love may not be sustainable as the energy eventually needs to be distributed to other aspects of life. Once the feelings change, people may think that something is wrong or maybe it's time to move on. Feelings serve different purposes at different stages of the relationships, and therefore they come in different intensities and forms.

The human spirit
The conscience

A man moved to another country with his wife and children. While in that country he fell in love with another woman. The woman demanded that the man must find a way of getting rid of his wife so he could marry her. Not knowing how to appropriately get rid of his wife, the man decided to hire an assassin to eliminate the wife and the children. He paid the assassin and created a trip so that when the assassin comes into the house he would not be there.

The assassin came. When he saw the woman and the children, his conscience convicted him. He could not kill them. They were innocent, he felt. Being a hard-core criminal, he was surprised at how soft he had become at this particular incident. He explained his mission to the frightened woman and children. He showed them the money her husband had paid him to kill them. He put them in his car and drove them through the night to the border and gave them the money he had been paid to use for transport on a bus to their country.

He went back to the man and told him that the mission had been accomplished and that he dumped all the dead bodies in a big river very far away where they could never be traced. The man immediately organized a trip to go to his home country to the family of the woman to notify them about the "tragedy." When he arrived, he was shocked to be welcomed by the "ghosts" of his wife and children. He had forgotten that *the person who pelts another with a pebble is asking for a rock in return.*

It was the conscience that made the assassin to change his mind. The conscience is the seat of one's values: the sense of what is right or wrong; or what is important and not important to the individual. If they would make a choice between one and the other, what would they choose? This reminds me of an incident that happened to me at a hotel in Kampala, Uganda. A girl knocked at the door of my room at about 7 pm. Not knowing who was knocking, I opened the door. Before I could ask how I could help her, she had already entered my room. I had previously met her briefly with a friend at the restaurant the previous evening, and that made me feel quite at ease with her. She started chatting with me, asking me where I came from, what I had come to do in Uganda, and how I was finding the country. After about an hour and a half she said she was leaving. I was very glad to hear that, but to my surprise she told me that I should pay her. I didn't understand. She said I should pay her for her time. Then I understood that I should have known that she was a prostitute, and that all along in the one and half hours she spent in the room we were not talking the same language. She explained to me that she had to bribe the guards to get access to my room, and that she had to pay them when she went back. I didn't see how that was my responsibility and why I should pay. She insisted, and threatened to create a scene. I was not ready for that type of embarrassment. I quickly paid her much less than what she was demanding, based on the fact that I did not get her services. She left.

In terms of values, we had different ones. Her value was money. Mine was moral responsibility. Because we had different values, we could not speak the same language.

For a person seeking spiritual progress, some of the values worthy of cultivating include:

- Acceptance of appropriate responsibility—the first responsibility is to seek and discover what it is one was put in this world for. Once the purpose is found, the second responsibility is to dedicate one's life to its fulfillment as one's mission. This means aligning all of one's life toward one's life mission. It is dedication to a conscious mission that makes possible the expression of one's full potential. It is also a clear mission that guides people on what their appropriate responsibilities are. *The poorest person on earth is not the one without money but the one without a vision.*
- Integrity—integrity means integration of all aspects of life for harmony. It also means ensuring that one's words and actions match. The goal of spirituality is to achieve integrity as a personal value and as a way of managing one's life. Integrity also means being open to both reason and faith. It means understanding that science or reason and faith are complementary. Science answers the "what" question of life while faith answers the "why" question of life.
- Openness to learning and avoiding bias—being open-minded is key for managing diversity. It helps one to better understand oneself and others. It also helps one in being centered in the sense that through it, one can decide what is important to keep on learning. This becomes an informed choice, rather than one made out of bias or prejudice.

It is the conscience that makes one human. Without the conscience, man would be an animal. The Greek word for conscience *suneides* means "to know the truth." Conscience differentiates between what we consider morally good or bad. It commends us when we are doing well and condemns us if we are doing wrong. The conscience is one's antennae that points to what one should or should not do in order to be free. The conscience is the spiritual eye. When

Christ said, "The eye is the lamp of the body. So if your eye is sound your entire body will be full of light. But if your eye is unsound your whole body will be full of darkness" (Amplified Bible, Matthew 6: 22 – 23), He was talking about the conscience. The word eye can be replaced with the word conscience. A healthy conscience gives light in terms of moral guidance while an unhealthy conscience is incapable of providing such guidance.

Seen from another angle, the conscience is neutral. It becomes good or evil if one lends oneself to good or evil respectively. Individuals must decide the type of conscience they desire. A good conscience breeds good. And a bad conscience breeds bad.

People of conviction have strong conscience. They will pay any price, even their lives, just not to betray their conscience. These are the ones who are willing to become prisoners of conscience. To them, their conscience is the scale of eternal justice.

One can make one's conscience strong by working on it to strengthen it. The way to strengthen it is to feed it with the right stuff.

Communion (ability to contact the spiritual)

Communion is a way of linking up to the spiritual world or transcendence, which makes accessing "supernatural wisdom" and guidance possible. Simply, it is the capacity for prayer. It is the faculty of communication that differentiates between prayer in religion and spiritual communication. Through this faculty one has the consciousness that he or she is talking to a Person in a living and dynamic relationship. It is this that makes memorized or written prayers ineffective and unnecessary.

In essence, spirituality can be summarized as communion with God and the effect this has on the person in terms of his or her conduct and relationships with others. It is communion that provides access to spiritual power.

Intuition

The intuition is the way of accessing "supernatural wisdom" (knowing without direct learning and guidance through the still small voice). The intuition is also referred to as the sixth sense. Hill (2003: 243) describes is as part of the subconscious mind (spirit) that can be referred to as the "creative imagination" and the "receiving set" through which ideas, plans, and thoughts flash into the mind. The flashes are also called "hunches" or "inspirations." They may also be referred to as "revelation." Covey describes it thus, "The value of one choice over another is not always completely rational or easily defensible, but it is discernible. With some form of intuition people know the 'right thing to do' and life is better off to the degree to which one learns to follow this 'guide.'"

A typical example of intuition at work that comes to my mind is a colleague—a young man staying in a rural area—who was suddenly awakened from sleep around 2 a.m. A *still small voice* within told him to get up and walk to his vegetable garden. He arrived just as some thieves were about to steal his vegetables, and he managed to chase them away. Another friend was driving somewhere when she got a strong feeling to visit her grandmother. She diverted and went there at 11 p.m.—a time she would not normally visit her grandmother. When she arrived she found her grandmother having problems with kidney stones and she had very high blood pressure. She immediately called for an ambulance, averting a possible major catastrophe. To this day, she says she does not know how she got the feeling but she is so happy she heeded it.

Intuition also provides guidance through what can be described as "hard to explain coincidences." It is said that coincidence is when God chooses to be anonymous.

A friend told me a story of how he traveled from his country to attend a conference in another country. The president of the country came to close the conference. Soon after the closure, my friend somehow found himself in a room where the president was giving government scholarships to some young people. He just happened to be there by accident. The president asked him why he was not lining up with the others. He explained that he was a foreigner; he was not from that country. "Are you not an African? This too is an African country. It doesn't matter, join your friends," the president told him. The president gave him a scholarship to study for a master's degree and a doctoral degree in America, and told him that he would give him a job of his choice in the country if he finished the doctoral course. When he finished, the president gave him a job. He moved his family from his country and became a citizen of that country.

I was traveling to Oxford, England for a writing project in 2008. On the plane from Amsterdam to London, I asked the flight attendant how I could connect from Heathrow airport to Oxford. Before she could answer, somebody I will call "an angel from Ghana" interjected and told me not to worry. When we arrived at the airport, he took me to the bus station. He paid a return fare for the bus for me though I insisted that I could pay for myself. The bus was to leave in an hour's time. He phoned his fiancée and told her to come and pick him up an hour later so he could see me off. He took me to a café and bought coffee and muffins for both of us. He helped me to get my luggage onto the bus. He gave me his number and made sure he waved me off as the bus left. This is what is called grace—unmerited favor.

The intuition can make one know somebody even if they have not met before. It is intuition that plays a key part in human connection at a deeper level. Through intuition, one can know without the aid of the five senses. This is the faculty that geniuses have learned to make use of. Great inventors, writers, artists, and others have learned to make use of their intuition.

The Spirit

Lisa Nichols, in the book, *The Secret*, makes a bold assertion that human beings are gods (2006: 164). At first I thought she was being blasphemous until I saw that Christ said the same in the New Testament (John 10:34) quoting Psalms 82: 6 (King James Version), "I have said you are gods, and all of you are children of the Most High." The word *god* has a small *g* meaning that it is a derivative of the God with a capital *g*. The god in man is the human spirit and it derives its power from the higher Spirit or the spiritual world. Without this connection the spirit is powerless because *to every human power there is a higher power*. With this connection, the power of the spirit is unfathomable. It is deeper and much more powerful than mind power.

I do not agree, however, with the assertion made in *The Secret* that as a human being, "you are God in a physical body. You are Spirit in the flesh. You are Eternal Life expressing itself as You. You are a cosmic being. You are all Power. You are all wisdom. You are intelligence. You are perfection. You are magnificence. You are the creator and You are creating the creation of You on this planet." (2006: 164). I believe that these attributes are reserved for the big Spirit or God and that the human being has the grace to manifest some of these attributes only by having his or her spirit empowered by the Spirit. The human spirit is not the Spirit. The human god is not God. In all traditions there is a deeper tradition that all inspiration flows from God, named or nameless, just as the sun is the ultimate source of all energy in nature (Adair, 2002: 318).

One of the principles of Alcoholics Anonymous is that before a person can be helped, he or she must acknowledge that he or she is an alcoholic and recognize that of himself or herself can do nothing. One must acknowledge that one cannot do anything about it because one has no power to do so and that one is defeated. When one accepts this view, one is in a position to receive help from other alcoholics and from the Higher Power—the Spirit of God.

The alcoholic must then be willing to depend on the Higher Power from Whom he or she will derive strengths that he or she does not possess (Peale, 1998: 282). The Higher Power or the Spirit is separate and independent of the human spirit. Just as the sun is the ultimate source of all physical energy, the Spirit is the ultimate source of all spiritual life and energy. The human spirit thrives as it depends on and draws upon the Spirit.

While it may be impossible to prove the existence of the Spirit or God, or indeed to comprehend all of His attributes, He can only be understood and known in terms of His relationship to human beings. In this sense, He is a Person. He is a Person separate from persons but relates with the persons. Buber (1987: 168) states that, "the description of God as a Person is indispensable for everyone who means by 'God' not a principle and not an idea but Him who—whatever else He may be—enters into a direct relation with us men in creative, revealing, and redeeming acts, and thus makes it possible for us to enter into a direct relation with Him." It is beyond the scope of this book, and indeed unnecessary to discuss what God's essential being is, except to emphasize that God is also a Person. This is the essence of the Christ in the Christian teaching—God has a human face is Christ and through Christ we can relate with Him as a Person. Christ is Emmanuel—God with us human beings. If human beings see Christ they see God and how He wants them to relate with Him and each other.

A distinction between a person and the Person is that though independent, a person is limited by the plurality of other independent persons. The Person, however, is the absolute Person experiencing no limitation. Being an absolute Person, He gives personal life, makes humans become capable of meeting with

Him and with one another but no limitation can come upon Him as the absolute Person, either from human beings or from their relationships with one another.

Buber (1987: 170) further observes that conversation between the person and the absolute Person, or the speech of the Person to a person, penetrates what happens in the life of each of us, and all that happens in the world around us, biographical and historical, and makes of it to the person instruction, a message and/or a demand, one happening after another, one situation after another is enabled and empowered by the personal speech of the Person to demand of the human person that he or she takes his or her stand and makes his or her decision. Many times, human beings think there is nothing to hear but the real problem is that they have closed their ears. Indeed, *God speaks in the parables of human activities and events* and *the Spirit speaks in the language of human beings.*

Conclusion

Understanding spiritual development involves a harmonized and integrated understanding of all of the aspects of the human being—the body, the mind and the spirit. It means working to strengthen the will—one's sense of vision and purpose—what is it that I will do in this world? Based on this, the will makes decisions that are aligned with this grand decision. The will is supported by the emotions and the intellect. The intellect provides the intellectual intelligence, and the emotions working in conjunction with the conscience provide emotional intelligence. Intellectual intelligence and emotional intelligence ensure that the decisions made are both ambitious and humane. The intuition ensures that the decisions made have a spiritual consideration.

A spiritual approach to organizational development involves working primarily with the organization's will—what is it that our organization will do in the world? What is our ultimate responsibility? This is the organization's sense of mission and purpose. It is a well articulated and internalized organizational purpose or mission that gives meaning to the people in the organization and those that they serve. The greatest contribution a leader can make to an organization is a strong sense of vision, mission, and purpose that will outlast him or her. A purposeless organization cannot go very far.

The purpose is fed by the organization's intellect and emotions. The organization's intellect is its capacity for learning and reflection. The organization makes effective decisions if they are based on its reflection and learning. Organizations with learning disabilities cannot go very far.

An organization's emotional intelligence is based on its conscience expressed in its values. A great need for many organizations today is to ensure that they are humane. It is values that create a humane climate in the organization.

CHAPTER 4: BEING, DOING, AND RELATIONSHIP

Introduction
In order to help individuals and organizations surface, identify, and confront their contradictions or shadows for deeper and more lasting change and effectiveness, it is important for the worker or change agent to cultivate his or her being, doing, and relationships.

Working with individuals and organizations can happen at three levels, since you can be a:

Conduit, who is able to identify and use the most appropriate tools available. One mostly relies on one's study and ability to pass on what one has read or studied.

Contextualizer, who is able to contextualize and use the best available tools. One mostly relies on reflection and learning from one's own practices.

Creator, who creates original tools that are best suited to the situation he or she is working with. He or she operates at the level of revelation and mostly relies on contemplation and meditation.

It is important to clarify that these three levels are not mutually exclusive. They are progressive. People move from being a conduit to a creator as they engage more and more consciously with their work. The person operating at the creator level is often more rigorous than those operating at the preceding levels. There is no success without sacrifice. The deeper the level of practice one wants, the greater the sacrifice will be required.

Being
To know whether or not one is spiritual, one has to simply look at the fruit one is producing and whether that fruit is a result of reliance on the Spirit or simply out of one's natural self. A spiritual person's fruit or overall impression is a result of his or her reliance on the Spirit. The work accomplished in an individual's life by the presence of the Spirit is love, joy (gladness), peace, patience, kindness, goodness (benevolence), faithfulness, gentleness (meekness, humility), and self-control (self-restraint). With a well-cultivated spirit, one impresses with joy, strength, wisdom, and power, which will radiate from the individual without any effort on his or her part. Though people may be unconscious of it, strong people will be drawn toward them, influence will be put into their hands. Outward events will shape themselves in accordance to one's cultivation of one's spirit. The question is not whether it is possible to get and practice these virtues without being spiritual, but whether it is possible to operate at a deep and fundamental level of required change without being spiritual.

Whether or not an individual can do work with spiritual effectiveness does not depend so much on his or her words or actions, but rather on what comes from him or her in terms of the overall impression. What emanates from the being or the spirit of the person is important to consider. This impression is what Ralph Waldo Emerson refers to as character. Of it he says, "Character is the reserved force that acts directly by presence, and without means." Deep, lasting effectiveness comes from one's spirit.

When we meet people, we generally have an impression about them, which can be good or bad. This impression does not come merely from the person's words or actions. There is a mysterious something that expresses itself while the person is speaking or acting. It is this something that gives the impression. What we sense in such moments is the person's most outstanding feature, which is the true nature of the person's being.

A non-spiritual person—one without intuitive capacity—will use his or her mind to contact people and therefore can only meet the people's minds, as he or she cannot reach their spirit. It is the characteristics of people's minds that may give one an overall impression. The person's strongest characteristics, whether spiritual or mental, are what will form a person's overall impression. The key question is: what impression do I make on others? The essence of character impression cannot be faked, at least in the long term, because *character is like a pregnancy—it cannot be hidden for long.*

The key need of a spiritual person is the release of his or her spirit. This is possible when a person's spirit is strong enough to break through the mind in terms of giving one the overall impression that they make on others. It is at this level that people can meet the individual's spirit and be touched and helped at that deeper level. It is at this level that one can be used as a channel of the life-giving energy that can result in people being served individually or collectively to be empowered in their quest for true purpose, meaning, or reality of life beyond the rational and at the intuitive level.

Without a proper ordering of the spirit and the mind, with the mind taking a higher position, the spirit cannot "break through" to make a spiritual impression on the people one interacts with. What is important is what comes from the person—what comes from his or her spirit, and not the words they speak or the actions they take. It is the spirit that gives a spiritual impression, which is the basis for true service.

Cultivating the being to release the spirit

According to Nee (1968: 84) there are two main means of cultivating the being for the release of the spirit in an individual. These are discipline and revelation. These two enable one's spirit to be in a position to give an overall impression, and enable one to offer spiritual service through one's work.

Disciplinary work refers to divinely ordered circumstances that come with the aim of breaking spiritual hindrances within an individual. They may come in the form of some difficulty in one's task environment, which may include a negative change in one's circumstances, an apparent failure, or a change in attitude toward one from some colleagues or friends. The aim is not to destroy or harm people, but to slow them so that they can reflect on these happenings and learn the lesson they are teaching. Suze Orman (2000: 319) advises thus: "If you can believe that somehow everything happens for the best reason and hold firm to this belief, especially during troubled times or when you undergo what appear to be setbacks in your life, then you will be able to draw the good out of any situation. You will be looking for the benefit, the hidden treasure, and you will be able to profit from even the toughest experience." It is through this learning that the individual can create more space for the operation of the spirit in his or her life.

The key challenge with this type of discipline in many people is that their levels of consciousness are too low to decipher the lesson being communicated to them. As a result, the discipline often lasts much longer than necessary. Spirituality is a progression throughout one's lifetime. Each divinely ordered discipline is meant to accomplish some spiritual purpose in an individual, with the aim of bringing him or her to the next level. Failure to decipher and use the lesson keeps individuals at one level for too long, hindering their spiritual growth and effectiveness.

The disciplining hand may last days, weeks, months, years, or even decades, depending on how conscious one is and how good one is at deciphering the lesson, and also the magnitude of the lesson to be learned.

Revelation refers to the Spirit graciously shining in an individual to enlighten them on some issue of spiritual significance. This light brings into sharp focus the issues that are hindering one's spiritual growth, even those little things one has overlooked and justified before. Revelation is a special endowment of deeper consciousness regarding the helping and hindering factors to one's spiritual growth. Revelation or enlightenment exposes one's true spiritual condition. The light of revelation both slays spiritual hindrances and enhances spiritual helping factors in an individual's life. Revelation is one of the key needs of a spiritual person. The effect of true enlightenment or revelation will leave its mark on the person for a long time, and sometimes for life.

In comparison, discipline is usually a slower process. It is repeated time and again, usually for a long time, before the individual gets the point and deals with the issues concerned. Discipline is usually initiated independently of the individual's effort. What is key is the individual's capacity to detect the lesson being communicated.

Revelation is usually much faster. This can take a few days or even a few minutes. Under the divine flashlight, one sees within a short time one's true spiritual condition. Revelation is usually triggered by some activity by the individual, which may include reading some inspiring material, listening to a speech, engaging in contemplation, or simply a sharing a conversation.

Releasing the spirit for spiritual effectiveness requires the ability to recognize the hand of discipline, and being open to revelation. Until the spirit is released, it cannot flow freely toward the people one is serving. It is the release of the spirit that supplies the real and deeper needs of the people. No spiritual work is as important as the ability to release one's spirit, and nothing can replace it. A real measure of a spiritual person is what comes from them, and whether they impress with their mind only, or also with their spirit. What comes from one's inner life matters more than what comes from one's mouth. This is the real measure of the value of spiritual work.

Doing

Spiritual perception or discernment is key for effectiveness in one's work. *The inside of a person is a sacred text.* In working with people, it is important to discern the spiritual climate and conditions one is dealing with. It is not possible to be truly effective and relevant without this ability. When we are doing organizational assessments or related assignments, for example, it is important to discern whether what people are saying is really so, and how much has been left unsaid. It is important to perceive the invisible characteristics of the organization. What is its culture? What are its values? What is the organizational climate like? And how are the relationships? Effectiveness is closely related to this ability. This does not mean undermining rational approaches, but it is important to note that though the tools and theories may be useful in providing frameworks for organizing data collection, analysis, and report writing, they may also be misleading—especially if one allows one's favorite frameworks to subjectively alter one's perception. In addition, no single theory can fully capture the range of conditions one is exposed to. Given the many tools and theories available, the worker would do better to heed Carl Jung's advice: "Learn your theories as well as you can, but put them aside when you touch the miracle of the living soul" (Belkin, 1988). A change agent's primary resources are their own inner resourcefulness and personal integrity (Kaplan, 1996: 120).

When the diagnosis is accurate, it is possible to prescribe the most effective and relevant solution. What works for one situation may not work for another. This is why the notion of "one size fits all" does not work. Organizations and individuals must be dealt with in their uniqueness and singularity, which can only be truly discerned at the spiritual level. Such discernment also enables the worker to determine whether or not he or she can be of help in intervening in a situation. No spiritual worker can deal with every condition they come across. Different people are gifted differently. That is why there are so many of us. Knowing one's place or niche is key for the effectiveness of every spiritual worker. It is also possible to fail to discern or "read" the true condition of the person or organization one is dealing with because it is beyond one's capacity to do so. Such situations call for humility from the worker. It is important in such instances to transfer such cases to those who are more able through their deeper experience or spiritual insight.

Spiritual discernment or perception also enables the worker to know whether the person or organization has come to him or to her for genuine help or to simply "use" him or her. This enables the worker to determine the true motive of the individual or client. In such a case, he or she should not waste time with those who are not genuine seekers. This is a higher level of intervention than merely dealing with organizations or people using only mental or mind understanding. It is the spirit that enables one to discern the real need of the person or the organization. The spiritual worker must be able to *"look at your children to see their questions before they ask them."* This should not be taken to mean that the people the spiritual worker is dealing with are children.

To be an effective instrument of diagnosing individuals' and organizations' conditions, the spiritual worker needs thorough training and strict discipline.

Whatever is untouched or not dealt with within one's own life cannot be touched or dealt with in the lives of those one is working with. One cannot give what one does not have. The more thoroughly one's own issues have been addressed, the more effective one's work will be. It is not possible to pretend. *Character is like pregnancy—you cannot hide it for long.* If the same condition in the person or organization one is working with also exists in the worker, he or she cannot "exorcise those demons." While it is possible for medical doctors to cure others without having to cure themselves first, the same is not possible in spiritual work. The worker must first heal himself before attempting to heal others. He cannot take people where he has not gone himself. This calls for thorough preparation to ensure genuine effectiveness. Intervening in other people's lives is an enormous responsibility that should not be taken lightly.

According to Nee (1968: 43) discerning the individual's or the organization's condition involves "listening to" and "observing" their most outstanding impression. Block (1996: 209) observes that "what truly matters in our lives is measured through conversation. Our dialogue with customers, employees, peers, and our own hearts is the most powerful source of data about where we stand." It is the impression that is being felt that reveals the condition. When the individual or organization's spirit is in a normal state, the feeling is peaceful and pure. With a well-cultivated spirit, one's impression will comprise joy, strength, and power, which will be radiated from the individual without any effort on his or her part. An abnormal state gives a feeling of uneasiness. The feeling the spirit gives is a mirror of the mental and physical conditions of the entity. Being able to touch a person or an organization's spirit like this makes it possible to know what their exact need is. To know a person or an organization, one must know them according to their spirit.

We know a person through listening and observing. We know a person through the words they speak, what they leave unsaid, and their body language. This calls for deep listening. It is important to listen to the content, the emotions, and the intent. This deep listening will reveal the person's spirit—for out of the abundance of the heart the mouth speaks. The spiritual worker must not let the content of the discussion or dialogue distract him or her from the emotions and intent, which reveal the spirit of the speaker. The ability to discern an individual's or an organization's spirit enables the Spirit to work through the spiritual worker's spirit to work out the eternal purposes in the life of the individual or the organization.

Cultivating spiritual consciousness

Becoming a spiritual person is a decision that an individual has to make. It does not just happen. There are a few things one needs to know and do to become a more spiritual person.

1. Spiritual people are not born spiritual. They make a conscious decision to become spiritual. Every spiritual person was once non-spiritual person. Every unfolding starts small and grows big with disciplined cultivation and nurturing.

2.   It is important to have a "mountaintop" experience. It is at the mountaintop where the individual meets or become consciously aware of his or her sense of purpose and the true meaning of their life. One climbs to the mountain oneself. No one can come with you. It is a solitary experience. No one can do it for another. This is called a place of one person. Napoleon Hill captured this well when he said: "Where you belong is as individual a place as you are as an individual person. There is a special place, a special job for each of us. Yours is not your neighbor's and your neighbor's is not yours." It is in this solitude that one consolidates and clarifies what their niche and contribution will be. *Life never overburdens a person.* It only expects of them what is within their niche. All great spiritual people have had a mountaintop experience.

3.   As an extension of the mountaintop experience, spiritual individuals usually go through a "wilderness" experience. This is a time of tests and temptations. Every great person passes through a wilderness experience. The Israelites went through the wilderness for 40 years, Moses fasted for 40 days, Christ was in the wilderness for 40 days and nights. The wilderness comes before breakthrough. The wilderness is a time for preparation for service to humanity. It is not possible to make a spiritually significant contribution without first going through the wilderness experience.

4.   A spiritual person will never walk alone. There will always be "divine connections." They will usually be connected to individuals and groups that will provide them with the spiritual and other support they need on their journey. They will meet people who will mentor, coach, guide, and support them. They will be divinely guided to meet the right people who will help them achieve their purpose. These people will guide and, if necessary, push the individual to where they belong and in so doing aligning the individual with his or her purpose. The person's concept of family expands beyond blood and marriage relations to embrace all people from all walks of life with whom he or she feels a deep sense of kinship through shared values, purposes, and causes.

5.   A mark of a truly spiritual person is their servant spirit. The person is comfortable doing the most basic manual work. This gives him or her humility. All great people are humble people. They can do the most basic and simple work often reserved for the lowest people in society without feeling demeaned in any way. The person recognizes that any greatness they may possess may not be wholly deserved. It is by grace.

6.   They have a deep relationship with the Spirit and recognize the divine source of their power and ability. As a result, they invest a lot of time in cultivating their spiritual relationships. Spiritual people may spend more time in cultivating their divine relationship than in the actual work they do. In other words, their relationship with the divine is more important than their work.

7. Spiritual people discern open doors. Prayers have to come to an end and work must be done. Spiritual people intuitively recognize opportunities and seize them. It is the responsibility of the individual not only to recognize but also to open doors of opportunity. There is a time for prayer and there is a time for action. There are doors that only God can open. Often these doors are too big for an individual to open alone. But there are also doors you must open alone—no one will open them for you. Some things must not be spiritualized; they must be dealt with physically and practically.

8. Boldness and acts of faith—all great people and spiritual people are risk takers. They are as bold as a lion. They are action-oriented people. They know that if they do not act, nothing will happen because initiative is the pass key that opens the door of opportunity.

The importance of consciousness in personal and organizational effectiveness cannot be overemphasized. Havel (1990: 14 – 15) observed that, "Consciousness precedes being and not the other way round...For this reason, the salvation of this human world lies nowhere else than in the human heart, in the human power to reflect, in human meekness and in human responsibility. Without a global revolution in the sphere of human consciousness, nothing will change for the better in the sphere of our being as humans, and the catastrophe toward which this world is headed—be it ecological, social, demographic or general breakdown of civilization—will be unavoidable." Consciousness of human responsibility is indispensable for the future of humanity and God is not in the habit of descending from heaven to solve man's problems especially those he can solve for himself. *God will only help one when one wakes up.* Over and over again we see individuals, organizations, even countries getting stuck because people are refusing to take responsibility for personal and organizational responsibility for personal, organizational or even national renewal. When responsibility is avoided no amount of external help can help.

Relationship
If there is one message that spirituality has it is that relationships and people are more important than things. Harmonious relationships form the basis for all development. *Two birds disputed about a kernel, when a third swooped down and carried it off.* This goes against much of the common thinking today especially in development work where "efficiency" and "results" override people and relationships. This has been called a "substantialist" mode of thought. Substantialist words include money, technical assistance, catalyst, aid architecture, incentives, targets, mechanisms, outcomes, vulnerable groups, etc., while relational words include patterns, systems, processes, waves, networks, emergent change, uncertainty, and relativity (Eyben, 2011: 28 – 30).

Aid conditionality, including imposing foreign cultures on dependent societies, is an example of the value attached to substantialist mode of thought. One thing that can be made out of this is the evident clash of culture between the West and Africa. It is very clear, for example, that governments in the West and those in Africa look at the issue of homosexuality differently. From an OD perspective, we look at this issue as one of culture and cultural differences. Issues of culture are very complex and deeply entrenched among people. Sensitivity of issues such as sex is even more complex. Issues of gender, for example, were relatively less complex and therefore much easier to be accepted because they made sense to the people. What has been considered "normal" regarding sexual practice among a people over 10,000 years cannot be changed overnight. The process cannot be hurried. What is needed is an adult-to-adult dialogue of cultures.

The connotation one gets now is that the West is in a hurry to see their culture triumph, with some Western governments insinuating, nay declaring, using their financial power to usurp African governments' sovereignty by tying their financial support to the governments' acceptance of homosexuality rights. The proverbs *a foreigner took over from the owner of the house* and *foreigners bear strange gifts to the host ring true*. From an OD and developmental perspective this is unfortunate, because if the West considers acceptance of homosexuality as part of development, it is well known that development cannot be imposed and neither can it be hurried. Development is a natural process and can only happen when people are ready. It does look like cultural sovereignty is at stake in Africa, one of the indicators of Africa's lack of economic independence for self-determination. *Only equals can be friends.*

What is more worrying is that instead of abating, substantialist thinking and practice are gaining ascendancy, alienating the human spirit further and further in personal and organizational life. In a day of tightening resources and the need for quick results, we run the risk of selling our souls to short-term survival at the expense of long-term viability and sustainability. In the heat of the moment, we run the risk of forgetting that it is possible to think about efficiency and results within a relational framework, if we can only allow for a little flexibility, creativity, and innovation. Funding partners need to reflect on the proverb, *do not give me a goat and hold on to its tail.* Recipient organizations and countries need to reflect on the proverbs, *if you borrow another person's legs, you will go where he directs you; others' ornaments tie the neck* and *the fly had its life before the dog had its wound.*

Conclusion
Effective work is not about one's competence only. It is more about one's relationships with other people. Make people feel unthreatened. Make them feel important. Ask them about their experiences. Show them you value them. Don't focus on yourself. Focus on them. Find out where they feel their weaknesses are and then gently put yourself into that space. Be interested in people beyond just business. The most important business is relationship building. Spirituality is about relationships. CDRA (2004: 17) emphasize this point when they note that "the task of the development practitioner is to intervene into the life of complex living systems in ways that shift relationships that define them. Our challenge is to help bring 'stuck' relationships that have ceased to develop back to movement toward healthy functioning. We are relationship workers." Brian Tracy (1993:

259) notes that "the most important and the most highly paid form of intelligence is social intelligence, the ability to get along well with other people. Fully 85 percent of your success in life is going to be determined by your social skills, by your ability to interact positively and effectively with others...learning how to develop and maintain superior human relationships can do more for your career and for your personal life than perhaps anything else you can accomplish."

Spirituality is not fuzzy, amorphous, and a bunch of rituals. It is normal life characterized by healthy relationships nurtured by an awakened human spirit.

CHAPTER 5: SPIRITUAL POWER

Introduction
Spiritual power emanates from a person's spirit. Through spiritual power, people exert influence by simply being who they are. Since spiritual power does not arise from political position or possession of money, a spiritually powerful person may be rich or poor. Riches or poverty do not affect one's power. But power feeds on power. Power tends to attract other forms of power. People with money and with political power will naturally be attracted to the spiritually powerful person. For this reason, a truly spiritual person is not likely to remain poor for long unless it is by conscious choice. Indeed, one of the biggest temptations a spiritual person watches against is the love of money and its corruptive power. The spiritual person who is immune to the love of money is truly powerful and spiritual. This, however, should not be taken to mean that being spiritual is synonymous with being poor. The point is the amount of money he or she has or does not have does not influence the spiritual person at all. He can be a billionaire or a pauper, but that does not change who he is.

As power feeds on power, or power attracts power, one's power may not be exclusive of other forms of power. It is possible to find in the same person spiritual power, political power, and financial power to varying degrees. It is the dominant power that one is identified with that describes what power they have, whether spiritual, financial, intellectual, or political. In my book, *Power and Influence: Self-Development Lessons from African Proverbs and Folktales,* I discuss these four types of power extensively. I discuss how to acquire them, how to use them, and also how one may lose them.

The state of humanity today suggests that minus cultivation of spiritual power, the prospects look quite grim. There is a big need in the world today for spiritual leadership.

The lives of great and spiritual men and women normally reveal a pattern of strategic timing as though providence has aligned the life of the man or woman with the course of the age to achieve some higher purpose (Mansfield, 2005: 200). Martin Luther King Jr. and Mahatma Gandhi are two individuals who in their lives recognized that the key challenge for many change efforts is that they do not go deep enough to effect fundamental change and that these efforts do not go deep enough to enable people to identify, surface, and confront their contradictions or shadows. They recognized the importance of spiritual insight or the spiritual dimension to the social and political issues they were dealing with. Throughout their lives they demonstrated that spiritual insight can effect change at a level that other approaches cannot reach.

Martin Luther King Jr.
Martin Luther King Jr. was born on January 15, 1929 in Atlanta, Georgia, U.S.A. He was a son of the Reverend Martin Luther King and Alberta Williams King. He was a prominent human rights and civil liberties activist in the mid-20th century America.

Spiritual and political evolution

The main influences on King's life were Howard Thurman, Mahatma Gandhi, and Bayard Rustin. Howard Thurman, civil rights leader, theologian, and educator, was King's early influence. As a student, King often visited Thurman for coaching and mentoring on civil rights activism. Thurman played a foundational role in King's formation as a civil liberties activist.

King adopted the concept of non-violence primarily through his readings of Gandhi. He read several books by and about Gandhi. He was encouraged by Bayard Rustin, who himself had studied Gandhi, to implement the philosophy of non-violence practically. King later declared that in his civil rights work, Christ provided the Spirit while Gandhi provided the strategy.

In 1959, King visited Gandhi's birthplace in India. Of that trip, King reflected:

> Since being in India, I am more convinced than ever before that the method of non-violent resistance is the most potent weapon available to oppressed people in the struggle for justice and human dignity. In a real sense Mahatma Gandhi embodied in his life certain universal principles that are inherent in the moral structure of the universe, and these principles are as inescapable as the law of gravity.

King was also influenced by the writings of the leading Protestant writers of the era including Paul Tillich, Reinhold Niebuhr, and Walter Rauschenbusch.

King described his childhood years as very happy ones. "The first 25 years of my life were very comfortable years, very happy years. I did not have to worry about anything...I went right through school and I never had to drop out to work or anything."

This comfort and happiness was not to last long. Things changed when he began to engage more consciously and seriously with issues of political and social justice.

Career

King's career as a civil rights leader began in 1955 when Mrs. Rosa Parks, a well-respected African American seamstress, refused to relinquish her seat in a bus to a white person as demanded by the law at that time. She was immediately arrested and convicted of violating the city's segregation law. The African American leaders in the city and their white sympathizers decided to fight the case in court. They also decided to organize themselves to boycott the buses as a way of forcing change to the oppressive law. This led to the birth of the Montgomery Improvement Association and King was made its first president.

King was elected president because he was seen as a better educated and articulate young man. He was also new on the scene. For these reasons, he could be expected to win adherents and minimize opposition to the boycott. His status as a religious leader of a relatively affluent congregation could attract support from the traditionally conservative clergy. They also thought that if the boycott failed, his stakes could not be as high as the other leaders.

King's power of connection through oratory was clearly distinguishable in the first address to the public on the boycott. In the words of his biographer, Taylor Branch, who chronicled the event:

> The boycott was on. King would work on his timing but his oratory had just made him forever a public figure. In the few short minutes of his first political address, a power of communication emerged from him that would speak inexorably to strangers who would both love and revile him like all prophets. Gardner 1996: 206.

That night, the man and the hour met and Martin Luther King Jr. King had entered into his destiny. From that moment, King had been thrust into leadership with others looking up to him for hope and direction.

King's vision, which guided his speeches, writing, and presence, was founded on four main elements:

1. The most dominant theme in his life was his Christianity. His life was shaped by the teachings and personalities of the Bible. The key personalities were Christ and Moses. He saw these as liberators of oppressed people. King's faith was beyond mere religion. He believed in a living and personal God. He believed in a God who could communicate with him directly concerning his calling and work. He spoke of an experience he had in 1957 after a period of uncertainty and doubt. "I could hear an inner voice saying to me, Martin Luther, Stand up for righteousness. Stand up for justice. Stand up for truth. And lo, I will be with you to the end of the times." (Phillips, 1998)

2. His experience with the African American church—being a son of a prominent pastor and with the church as the only truly influential institution of the African American community at that time – he had a head start in leadership. He grew up in the church and became a pastor at a young age. He cultivated his public speaking skills there.

3. King's message was built primarily on his Christian tradition but also accommodated other traditions, including Catholic, Jewish, Islamic, and Eastern religious traditions.

4. He had a deep commitment to the principal democratic ideas and ideals upon which America had been founded.

King recognized that his leadership was not entirely a matter of personal choice. Of this he said:

> I realized that the choice leaves your hands. The people expect you to give them leadership. You see them growing as they move into action, and then you know you no longer have a choice, you cannot decide to stay in or out. You must stay in it.

King's call was consolidated through an experience he had after a lot of threats on his life and many frustrations. He described it thus:

And I sat at that table thinking about that little girl and thinking about the fact that she could be taken away from me any minute. And I started thinking about a dedicated, devoted and loyal wife who was over there asleep...and I got to the point that I could not take it anymore. I was weak.

And I discovered that religion had to become real to me, and I had to know God for myself. And I bowed down over that cup of coffee. I never will forget it ...I prayed a prayer, and I prayed out loud that night. I said, Lord, I am down here trying to do what is right, I think I am right. I think the cause we represent is right. But Lord, I must confess that I am weak now. I am faltering. I am losing my courage.

And it seemed at that moment that I could hear an inner voice saying, 'Martin Luther, stand up for righteousness. Stand up for justice. Stand up for truth. And lo I will be with you, even until the end of times.'...I heard the voice of Jesus saying still to fight on. He promised never to leave me, never to leave me alone. No never alone, never alone. He promised never to leave me, never to leave me alone (Yancey, 2007: 20).

This became King's bedrock of personal faith that enabled him to face all the crises of his life.

Achievements

King won two main wars and several battles. His battles were mostly the protest activities and marches of the early 1960s. These took place in Montgomery, Alabama, Albany, Georgia, and Birmingham, Alabama. These efforts scored some modest success.

King's most impactful efforts were the two events that happened in 1963. These were the letter he wrote from a Birmingham jail, and his famous "I have a dream" speech on August 28, 1963 during the March on Washington campaign.

King wrote in response to some white clergymen who accused him and his movement. The clergymen had stated that the demonstrations were counter-productive and they urged the African Americans to be more patient instead. The letter from Birmingham represents the most comprehensive statement of King's position—the issues he was addressing and at the highest point of his power and influence. In the letter, King refuted the allegation that the demonstrations were counter-productive and argued that waiting or being patient was not the answer as the African Americans had already waited for 340 years in vain. In the 20-page letter, he comprehensively presented the history of the African American people and charted the needed future action for self-liberation. This document is still regarded by many as a threshold statement of the American creed.

The March on Washington speech gave King the most visibility. His "I have a dream" speech has been chronicled as one of the best and most powerful speeches of the 20th century. The central focus of the speech was to dramatize the oppressive situation of the African American people in America. His aim was to force white America to surface its contradictions and confront its shadows.

King became the youngest recipient of the Nobel Peace Prize in 1964, and in 1965 was announced as *Time Magazine*'s Man of the Year.

King's strength emanated from integrating a powerful visionary message with the personification or embodiment of that message. King often had to fast for several days in order to achieve the spiritual discipline necessary for him to forgive his enemies. He explained, "We love men not because we like them, not because their ways appeal to us, not even because they possess some kind of divine spark. We love every man because God loves him." Yancey, 200: 281.

King demonstrated courage by leading in front, defying many threats, arrests and attempts on his life. This enabled him to connect deeply with the people. Through his message and personification he helped to provide a feeling of identity for the African American people in particular and dispossessed people or oppressed people in general. Since his power emanated primarily from his being, his contribution seems to have had no predecessor or successor.

King was assassinated on April 4, 1968 in Memphis, Tennessee, where he had gone to support striking African American sanitary workers. He died as a victim of the very evil force he had dedicated his life to fight against.

A few years before his death, King was asked about mistakes he had made. He replied, "Well, the most pervasive mistake I have made was in believing that because our cause was just, we could be sure that the white ministers of the South, once their Christian consciences were challenged, would rise to our aid. I felt that the white ministers would take over our cause to the white power structures. I ended up, of course, chastened and disillusioned. As our movement unfolded, and direct appeals were made to white ministers, most folded their hands and some even took stands against us" (Yancey, 2007: 38).

King's legacy

King's central message was that moral change is not accomplished through immoral means. He believed that non-violence was the only way that could keep the oppressed from becoming like the oppressor—the tendency of the oppressed becoming a mirror image of the oppressors they overthrow.

King's main legacy was to secure progress for civil rights, especially among African Americans, in the United States. This has enabled more African Americans to realize their potential. Martin Luther King was a great influence and motivation for Barak Obama—the first African American President of the United States.

Outside America, King's legacy was a great influence to the black consciousness movement and the civil rights movement in South Africa, which eventually brought down the apartheid regime and introduced a peaceful transition to a black majority rule.

A few months before his death, King spoke of how he wanted to be remembered.

I would like somebody to mention that day that Martin Luther King Jr., tried to live his life serving others. I would like for somebody to say that day that Martin Luther King tried to help somebody.

I want you to say that I tried to be right on the war question. I want you to be able to say that day that I tried to feed the hungry. I want you to be able to say that I did try in my life to clothe those who were naked. I want you to say that day that I did try in my life to visit those who were in prison. And I want you to say that I tried to love and serve humanity.

Yes, if you want to say that I was a drum major, say that I was a drum major for justice. Say that I was a drum major for peace. I was a drum major for righteousness. And all the other shallow things will not matter. (Carson, 1998:365 – 366)

Hodgson (2009: 230) concludes his book *Martin Luther King* by noting that "His influence was far more positive than negative. King's campaign, his great speeches, his letter from Birmingham jail and personal example; not to mention his death, had the cumulative effect of making a serious defense of the racial status quo untenable. In that sense, he was not just the most brilliant orator of his age; he was also one of its most influential teachers."

Martin Luther King is the only African American and clergyman to be honored with a national holiday in America.

Mahatma Gandhi

Born on October 2, 1869, Mahatma Gandhi was the pre-eminent political and ideological leader during India's struggle for independence from British colonial rule. Gandhi's awakening to his call started in South Africa, where Africans and Indians faced discrimination from the white minority rule. This experience with racism, prejudice, and injustice made him begin to question his place in society and his people's standing in the British Empire. He came to the conclusion that the West had forfeited its ability to lead the human race, and that the West represented a future of decadence, materialism, and armed conflict. He looked for a new way based on spiritual, not material strength. (Yancey, 2007: 145).

Gandhi first adopted his still-evolving methodology of non-violence in Johannesburg, which led over seven years to thousands of Indians being jailed and flogged for striking, refusing to register, burning their registration cards, or engaging in other forms of non-violent resistance. It was during this period that Gandhi's idea of non-violence took shape. Gandhi was greatly influenced by philosophers such as Henry David Thoreau, John Ruskin, and Leo Tolstoy. In essence, Gandhi's philosophy of non-violence involved people who feel oppressed or discriminated non-violently refusing to obey unjust laws and being prepared to accept any consequences—ranging from arrest to death.

Principles, practices, and beliefs
Truth and non-violence

Gandhi dedicated his life to the wider purpose of discovering truth. He tried to achieve this by learning from his own mistakes and conducting experiments on himself. Gandhi believed that the most important battle to fight was overcoming his own demons, fears, and insecurities. Gandhi would arise daily at

2 a.m. to read from Hindu or Christian scriptures and say prayers. He would stay the next few hours answering correspondence, and then he would do his ritual ablutions (Yancey, 2007: 144).

Gandhi also linked truth to non-violence. He referred to non-violence as "silent force" or "soul force," which arms the individual with soul power rather than physical power. He told his disciples to fight with the weapons of prayer, fasting, prison terms, and bruises from beatings from the police. Prison was no threat to Gandhi and his followers. In all, he spent 2,338 days in jails.

Gandhi was the first person to apply the principle of non-violence in the political field on a large scale. He faced all the crises he encountered with this "soul force" or the power of human spirituality. He believed the principles of non-violence could be adopted and practiced even by governments, the police, and armies. He, however, realized that this level of non-violence practice required incredible faith and courage, which he believed not many people possessed. Personally, his faith in non-violence was inflexible. During World War II, he counseled first the Ethiopians invaded by the Nazi army, then the Jews, then Great Britain, to invite their enemies and stand before the slaughter with serenity and a clear conscience. He told his followers that if an atom bomb were dropped on India they should look up; watching without fear, praying for the pilot. (Yancey, 2007: 149).

Vegetarianism

Vegetarianism was one of the tenets of Gandhi's life-long philosophy. He was a strict vegetarian, though later in life he could take goat milk on advice from a doctor. He wrote a book on the moral basis of vegetarianism. He had a wide network and contacts with the prominent vegetarians of his time. He believed that vegetarian diets adequately meet the body's dietary requirements, and also that they are generally more economical than meat diets. At a time when many Indians had low incomes, vegetarianism was seen not only as a spiritual practice but also a practical one.

Basic education

Gandhi believed that knowledge and work are not separate. He was a very strong advocate of basic education for all. After observing the English basic educational system and its interaction with colonialism, he saw the danger of education for the Indian children creating an alienating effect and creating "career-based thinking"; and also the disdain of manual work, the development of a new elite class and increasing problems of industrialization and urbanization. His focus was to emphasize life-long character of education, social character, and its form as a holistic process. He defined education as, "the moral development of the person"—meaning a life-long process.

Sexuality

Gandhi saw sexual abstinence as a means of coming close to God and as a key foundation for self-realization. He became celibate at the age of 36 while still married. He saw celibacy as playing a key role in one's control of the senses in thought, word, and deed. He tested his vow of chastity by sleeping in his room together with naked young women.

Simplicity

Gandhi strongly believed that a person involved in public life should lead a simple life. He gave up wearing western-style clothing. He associated this with wealth and success. He also renounced the western lifestyle in general. He dressed to identify with the poorest people in India, advocating for the use of home-spun cloth. He gave up unnecessary expenditure embracing a simple lifestyle and washing his own clothes. He called this practice "reducing himself to zero." He told his disciples to be ready to sleep upon the bare floor, wear course cloth, get up at unusually early hours, eat simple food and even clean their own toilets.

He spent one day each week in silence believing that silence brought him inner peace and made him a better listener. On such days he communicated with others by writing on paper. At some point in his life he refused to read newspapers claiming that the turmoil in the state of the world affairs caused him more confusion in his own inner self.

Gandhi believed that what the eyes are for the outer world, fasts are for the inner world. He thought that fasts conduced to mental ascendancy over the body (Fischer, 1997: 295).

Faith

Gandhi was an avid theologian and he read extensively about all of the major religions. He believed that the core of every religion was truth and love. He questioned what he saw as hypocrisy, malpractices, and dogma in all religions—including his own. He was a tireless advocate for social reform in religions. Later in life he used to say that he was Hindu, Christian, Muslim, Buddhist, and Jew. He also had an interest in theosophy. He identified with the theosophist message of the "universal brotherhood of man and the need for tolerance."

Self rule

Gandhi was a strong believer of participatory leadership and governance. He believed that all people, everybody in society, must be consulted before major decisions are made. He believed that true self-rule in a country means that every person rules him or herself, and that there is no state that enforces laws upon the people. Rather than a system in which rights are enforced by a higher authority, people are self-governed by mutual responsibilities. He believed more in human duties than in human rights. Gandhi also believed that national independence meant the existence of numerous self-sufficient, small communities that rule themselves without hindrance from others and without hindering others. He did not have faith in the British-styled Parliamentary system, and had plans to dissolve the Congress Party and introduce a system of direct democracy.

Gandhi summarized his beliefs in three points, which he credited to the Victorian author John Ruskin: 1. the good of the individual is contained in the good of all; 2. a lawyer's work has the same value as a barber's inasmuch as all persons have the same right of earning their livelihood from their work; and 3. a life of labor such as that of the tiller of the soil and a handicraftsman is the life worth living. He sought ways to put these principles into practice. In major cities, he preferred staying with sweepers rather than at a hotel. He would use a pencil until it was reduced to an ungrippable stub, out of respect for the person who made that pencil. He insisted on traveling third class on trains, explaining that he did so because there was no fourth class (Yancey, 2007: 151).

Gandhi's legacy

Gandhi is respected in India as a prominent 20th century leader. His greatest achievement was inspiring people around the world to the belief that it is possible for dispossessed and oppressed people to resist injustice in a dignified manner without counter attack and in a way that resolutions arrived at may empower all concerned. Gandhi did not only call for resolution of conflicts through peaceful means, he also developed the method to reach this aim.

Martin Luther King's most significant influence was Gandhi. He adopted and contextualized the principles of non-violence in America with some significant success. He declared that Christ gave the Spirit while Gandhi gave the strategy to the movement.

The United Nations General Assembly declared October 2 (Gandhi's birthday) as the International Day of Non-violence. January 30 (the day Gandhi was assassinated) is observed as the day of Non-violence and Peace in schools in many countries.

Time Magazine named Gandhi "Man of the Year" in 1930. In 1999 *Time Magazine* named Gandhi as a runner up to Albert Einstein as "Person of the Century." The 14th Dalai Lama, Lech Walesa, Martin Luther King Jr., Cesar Chavez, Aung Suu Kyi, Benigno Aquino Jr.; Desmond Tutu, and Nelson Mandela have been named as "Children of Gandhi" by *Time Magazine*. They have also been named his spiritual heirs to non-violence.

Lessons on spirituality

A number of lessons on spirituality can be drawn from the two case studies above. These include:

Spirituality and peace—Positive spirituality promotes peace and harmony. Martin Luther King and Mahatma Gandhi dedicated their lives to implementing peaceful means in their pursuit for social and political justice. Even in the face of great provocation they did not resort to violence in the realization that violence breeds only more violence. Truly spiritually powerful people are peaceful people. Martin Luther King used to say, "When evil men plot, good men must plan. When evil men burn and bomb, good men must build and bind" (Phillips, 1998).

Spirituality and contribution—the purpose of spiritual power is contribution to humanity. Spiritual people seek power not for personal interest but for enhancing humanity. They do not seek power for money or personal recognition but for contribution. People like Mahatma Gandhi and Martin Luther King have a deep commitment to the betterment of humanity to the extent of sacrificing so much, including their own lives. Spiritual people depend on divine providence and also the primacy of human agency. Martin Luther King observed that, "human progress is neither automatic or inevitable...even a surface look at history reveals that no social advance rolls in on the wheels of inevitability; it comes through the tireless efforts and persistent work of dedicated individuals. Without this hard work, time itself becomes an ally of the primitive forces of irrational emotionalism and social stagnation" (Washington, 1991: 104).

Belief in a personal God—Most spiritual people derive their energy and drive from a strong belief in a personal God. Unlike the God of religion who stays primarily in heaven, their God lives within them—in their spirits. They are driven by the conviction that human life has a meaning and that this meaning is ascribed by God. They believe that human beings are the highest of God's creation and that each human life has within it a divine purpose. They believe in a God who loves His people and is willing to liberate them from oppression. They do not believe in a historical God. They believe in a God who is active in everyday affairs of the world and individuals. They believe that they are instruments that God uses to carry out his purposes in the lives of people and in the affairs of the world.

Reality of good and evil—spiritual people believe at a conscious level in the reality of the ongoing cosmic war between good and evil. Siding with good, their lives become one of a continuous spiritual warfare against evil to the end of their lives. Every time an individual sets out to make a significant contribution to humanity, they declare war against the spiritual forces of evil and they should expect retaliation. Both Mahatma Gandhi and Martin Luther King Jr. suffered in various ways all their lives, including jailings, attempts on their lives, bombing of their homes, and finally paying with their lives for the simple reason that they were trying to make a positive contribution to humanity. They were dearly loved by good people and they were fiercely hated by evil people. Spiritual power is for spiritual warfare. Human beings cannot do much against evil if they do not have spiritual power.

Spiritual power and legacy—the spiritual person does not live only for today. He or she makes provisions for tomorrow and any emergency that may arise. They recognize their talents and invest them to enhance humanity. They identify their niche and build power around it. They do not try to do everything. They work only with their gifts and strengths and let others do the rest. They do not compare themselves to or compete with anybody else.

Unlike monetary and political power, genuine spiritual power is eternal and divine in its character. It transcends one's physical life. Though they died many years ago, Gandhi and King are still influencing humanity positively today. The world is a better place because they lived. Even in death their power cannot be effaced. Their vision and message transcended their own physical lives. In addition, their message was basically a human message and not only for their specific groups or people. Their message left a big challenge to the world that even today the whole of humanity is still striving to understand and effectively implement.

Spirituality and simplicity—the central focus of spiritual people is to make a positive contribution to humanity. They are not motivated by the need to make money or to gain social recognition. They therefore generally live a simple life and avoid any excesses. Spirituality does not espouse or encourage poverty. It discourages greed. A spiritual person does not own anything. Everything spiritual people have is seen as being given to them in trust, for divine or higher purposes. They see themselves as stewards.

Spiritual people side and identify with the poor and oppressed. This does not mean that they should become poor themselves, but they strive to become models for the people by not walking too far away from them in lifestyle, accumulation of resources, or recognition.

Spirituality and myths—spiritual people are real people and they live real lives. Though they spend more time cultivating or nurturing their spirituality, they are not mythical or mystical. They are people who are able to combine reason and faith for synergy. They are not too steeped toward spirituality to the extent of becoming too heavenly minded for earthly relevance. It is said of Hudson Taylor, a spiritual giant and a British missionary to China in the 19th century:

Hudson Taylor was no recluse. He was a father of a family, and one who bore large responsibilities. Intensely practical, he lived a life of constant change among all sorts and conditions of men. He was a giant in strength, no Atlas to bear the world upon his shoulders. Small in stature and far from strong, he had always to face physical limitations...he became a hard worker and an efficient medical man; he was able to care for a baby, cook a dinner, keep accounts, and comfort the sick and sorrowing; no less than to originate great enterprises and afford spiritual leadership to thoughtful men and women the wide world over (Taylor, 1987: 13).

Gandhi emphasized that he never heard a voice, saw a vision, or had some recognized experience of God. His guide was reason on the wing of faith (Fischer, 1997: 307).

The real value of spirituality is balance—the ability to look at any situation with a sober and unbiased mind and act in the most reasonable manner. Spiritual people recognize, as in the words of Nelson Mandela, that "a good head and a good heart make a formidable combination." They are practical.

A person who neglects his or her personal responsibilities because he or she is attending to his or her spiritual duties is not a truly spiritual person. Both Mahatma Gandhi and Martin Luther King did not give spiritual directives to the people and asked them to go and carry them out while they remained indoors attending to their spiritual duties. They led in front of the people. They led by example. They led real and balanced lives. They had children to raise, they had friends to attend to, and to a great extent they faced the pressure of balancing work and life. Martin Luther King harbored thoughts of becoming a university professor if and when the turmoil of the civil rights movement ended. They were careful *"not to invoke divine favors and forget to cultivate your fields"* and to realize that *God gave us brains to use.*

Spirituality and perfection—related to the above point, spiritual people are not spirits. They are human and therefore are not perfect. The only difference with the others is that they strive more toward their own perfection because they know that their ability to be a channel of spiritual power is greatly linked to their spiritual condition. Both Martin Luther King and Mahatma Gandhi had some questionable relationships with women deemed by some to have undermined their moral standing. This, however, did not dim their overall legacy and impact. Many people are under the illusion that spiritual people or spiritual leaders are as perfect as angels and judge them harshly when they fall. Spiritual people are not spirits. They are human. They are neither angels nor perfect. The difference is that they try to do something about their imperfections. A woman brought her young son to Gandhi asking him to tell the boy to stop eating sugar because she believed it was not good for his health. She said the boy would not listen to her but she believed that he would listen if Gandhi spoke with him. Gandhi told the woman to come back with her son after one week. When they came back Gandhi talked with the boy and asked him to stop eating sugar. The mother wondered why she had to come back after one week for Gandhi to tell her son to stop eating sugar. Gandhi explained that he asked her and her son to come back after one week because when they came the previous week, he himself was also eating sugar. He felt it would not be right for him to tell the boy to stop eating sugar when he himself was doing the same.

Conclusion

Of the lives of Martin Luther King and Gandhi it can be said that *"when God wills an event to occur, He sets the causes that lead to it."* They lived at times when the world needed some fundamental changes and they played a key role in bringing about that change. Despite the apparent helplessness and hopelessness of their situations, they never became despondent and gave up. They believed that *the pillar of the world is hope.* Despite encountering some setbacks they kept on because they believed that *an elephant does not die of a broken rib*—meaning that a strong person does not lose heart because of a single of a few misfortunes; they also believed that *people throw assegais at an elephant from all sides, the lion does not turn back when a small dog barks; and people only throw stones at trees that have edible fruit* meaning that a big person must experience a lot of opposition.

Of son of men like Martin Luther King and Gandhi, like a few others of them, it can also be said as was said of the Son of Man long ago, "A prophet powerful in speech and action before God and the whole people; how our chief priests and rulers handed him over to be sentenced to death and crucified him."

Men and women of real spiritual power and influence are few. They are few because not many people are prepared to make the sacrifice required for the acquisition of (spiritual) power and influence. Even fewer men and women are willing to build their character to a level congruent with the level of power and influence that they desire.

People are often led to causes and often become committed to great ideas through persons who personify those ideas. They have to find the embodiment of the ideas in flesh and blood in order to commit themselves to it (Phillips, 1998: 1). The ability to transform relationships and to help individuals and organizations identify, surface, and confront their contradictions or shadows for deeper and lasting change is dependent on the change agent's willingness to sacrifice and building their character to a level that is congruent to the level of power and influence they desire.

CHAPTER 6: STAGES OF SPIRITUAL DEVELOPMENT

Introduction

Spirituality is an unfolding characterized by increasing consciousness. Human consciousness moves from biological to psychological through to spiritual awareness. Different individuals are at different stages of their spiritual evolution. The stages of spiritual evolution include: spiritual unconsciousness, religious, seekers, personally spiritually conscious, and spiritual change agents. The reality of the spiritual dimension opens up to the individual at the personally spiritually conscious stage. The ability to challenge individuals and organizations to identify, surface, and confront their contradictions or shadows for deeper change depends to a great degree on the change agent's level of consciousness or their stage of spiritual development. Deeper spiritual insight comes with deeper levels of spiritual consciousness.

Spiritually unconscious stage

Spiritually unconscious people live exclusively in the physical and mental worlds. To them, the spiritual does not exist. To them, life is matter and energy. There is nothing beyond biology and psychology, and everything can be explained this way. Man is the center of the universe. They refuse to accept that *some secrets of life can never be deciphered.*

Usually having a feeling of self-sufficiency and independence many individual may not see the added value spirituality may add to their lives. *Unless one becomes needy, they may not know God.* This is why many individuals will only turn to spirituality much later in their lives when they come face to face with the issues of the uncertainty of life and the inevitability of their own death and what it means.

The spiritually unconscious are children in a spiritual sense. I remember my daughter at the age of 11 asking me after we had returned from a trip to another country, why she did not see God's house in the sky when we were in the plane. I understood her question very well because in my vernacular, sky and heaven are often used interchangeably. My other child asked me the other day, "Dad, they say that God holds this world in His hands, does He not get tired? The world is very big, it must be heavy." A friend's toddler in Kenya asked her concerning the famine in Somalia and the northern part of Kenya in 2011, "Mum, what happened? Does it mean that those people asked God to give them food and God refused to give them the food?"

Children are less restricted in asking questions about spirituality than are adults. This is an attribute adults would do well not to lose, for questions are an indicator of consciousness. The problem with many spiritually unconscious people is that they let the questions block their journey of spiritual discovery rather than using them as stepping-stones. *To deny God's existence is like jumping with your eyes closed.*

Religious stage

Religious people's worldview includes the spiritual realm. This is based on teachings set forth in holy books. At this stage the individual begins to recognize that *ignorance precedes knowledge and* that *too much knowledge obscures wisdom.*

Religion basically involves following rules and rituals with the aim of reaching out to God and meeting His requirements. The God of religion is usually a historical God. He spoke in the past and set His rules and rituals that must be followed. He does not speak anymore today, especially to individuals. His words are contained in His book. Religion emphasizes a God who lives in heaven while spirituality emphasizes the God who lives within the individual.

The typical religious person does not have a conscious personal relationship with his or her God. He is a group God who can be accessed through religious practices and rituals. Religious people do not expect God to speak to them personally; they do not expect to hear the voice of God. The concept of a dynamic and living relationship between the individual and God does not exist in a typical religion.

I heard a group of young people on the radio declaring that God plays no part whatsoever in their lives. Many people may not be courageous enough to put it this way. But the God who is locked in the pages of the holy books does not play much role in their lives, except by providing general guidelines of life and some promises for the hereafter. Many professionals are not impressed with such a God. Many professionals recognize their limitations in reaching out to humanity and that they need an active power that can intervene in human affairs and one that is active in their day-to-day lives. They need a power they can relate with in a living relationship. They need a power that can add value to their efforts. They need a living person-to-Person relationship. This Person is usually not found in religion. He is found in spirituality. This is why Eastern religions, which offer forms of spirituality, are making great inroads in the Western world, and in many cases are replacing traditional organized religion.

Seekers

Seekers are people who have failed to find meaning in religion. They find religion unsatisfactory in their quest for spirituality. At this stage, *what is sacred is a secret to many.* These are mostly thinkers who require adequate explanations for the big issues of life, like the purpose and meaning of life, and they are not satisfied by the answers given by religion. Many professional people fall in this category. At this stage, an individual questions whether such a thing as spirituality does exist, or it is just an imagination. And in case it does exist, does it really matter, or it is it something that can be ignored without any implications? Some individuals become destructive by discrediting anything religious or spiritual.

Dissatisfied with religion, many seekers decide to go back to the spiritually unconscious stage. Others decide to stay on in religion but not for spiritual reasons. They may stay on for social reasons. "Losing one's faith" is a common phenomenon at this stage. Many seekers have adopted a humanistic view of life—the belief in human reasoning rather than faith in the divine.

Open-minded seekers still have space to explore the spiritual. For the objective seeker, the battle between reason and faith is fiercest at this stage. A major issue a seeker strives with is his own sense of knowledge and intelligence. Being at the peak or high point of their professional careers, they wonder, "I am a very knowledgeable person. I am an expert in my field. Most of the things I was supposed to know I know. If this spirituality stuff was real, how come up to now I don't know about it. It must therefore not be real and if it is real it must be not very important." This thinking blocks learning and development. If reason wins, the seeker may abandon his or her journey of spiritual evolution. If faith wins, they may shift to the next stage. Many thinking people recognize their spiritual need. The challenge is that they do not find it in religion. This is why the search for spirituality is great today. Religion has a role to play. The challenge is when it suffocates rather than nurture spirituality.

Personally spiritually conscious
At this stage the reality of the spiritual dimension dawns on the individual. For the first time he or she realizes that *there is a whole world behind the invisible.* It is at this stage that the individual "crosses over" to the other side, becoming conscious that he or she is more than just a biological and psychological being. He recognizes that he is also a spiritual being. He also recognizes that *God is the contemporary of everything* and that *the creature is not greater than the Creator.* This is what in the Christian teaching is called the "new birth" experience. Just as it is natural for all human beings to seek physical and psychological relationships, it also becomes natural for the individual, at this stage, to seek spiritual relationships. Just as the river seeks the sea, one's spirit will naturally seek the Spirit. This is what Martin Buber calls the "I-Thou" relationship, which he contrasts with the "I-It" relationship. It is also at this stage when the person may consider the issue of a personal God. From a professional point of view, the issue may not be so much about whether God exists or not, for the existence of God cannot be proved. He can only be known by revelation or a deeper consciousness. The issue is whether or not spirituality adds value. But spirituality cannot be divorced from the supernatural, whether that supernatural is God or otherwise. The concept of God simplifies spirituality, because now one is talking about a Person and a relationship rather than about abstractions. God gives spirituality a face. Only the God of spirituality and not religion can do this. For some people, the simplicity to believe in a God requires a lot of courage and humility.

At this stage, the spiritually conscious is mostly a spiritual baby. He or she is mostly concerned about his or her spiritual well being—living a life of love and gratitude, living a well-balanced and integrated life—as in the words of one person I interviewed, "Spirituality is integrating the various aspects of myself and my life to navigate a meaningful path in the world of my journey of life." Spirituality is seen as a way of coping with pressures, uncertainties, and self-doubts. It is also seen as a way of maintaining perspective—the ability to see the bigger picture of life, society, destiny, and history. But all of these revolve around the self. This is "spirituality for me." His or her spirituality is purely a private thing. People at this stage may begin to integrate the sacred and the secular in their lives and the difference between the two blurs.

Spiritual change agents

These are people who have grown beyond "spirituality for me" to "spirituality for others." Their lives and professions consciously become channels through which spiritual power flows to bring about needed change and improvements in their environment and the people they relate with. At this stage one discovers that human beings are only instruments through which higher powers are projecting themselves and they take a conscious decision to let the power of good rather than evil to flow through them. These are the people whose professions and careers are transformed into callings. They are also conscious that if there is a calling there must be a caller—a higher power that is higher than themselves. These are shapers of society and the makers of history. Their power is based on the relationship with the source of power. They are given the keys that whatsoever they bind on earth is bound in heaven and whatsoever they loose on earth is loosed in heaven. Their power is recognized in heaven, on earth, and in hell.

Margaret Wheatley (2010: 23) calls these people "spiritual warriors." Of them she says:

> Spiritual warriors are those who are brave…they never use aggression or violence to accomplish their work. The skills that give them power are compassion and insight. It takes years of practice and discipline to cultivate these and a strong conviction that these are the skills most needed. Those who devote the time and exert the discipline to acquire these skills must trust themselves to be of service to this troubled time.

There is certain power that characterizes world shapers like Nelson Mandela, Martin Luther King Jr., Steve Biko, Mahatma Gandhi, Marcus Garvey, and Peter Drucker, among many others. It is not their money. It is not their intellect. It is not their political power. It is something deeper. It is the power of spiritual change agency for service to humanity. This is the experience that is called, "the baptism in the Holy Spirit and power" in the Christian teaching. Spiritual change agents maximize their human potential. They live a full life where a full life does not necessarily mean living a long life but accomplishing their life purpose.

To spiritual change agents the spiritual dimension is as vivid as the physical dimension. One of the spiritual men I know told me the story of his life's spiritual journey, which I found to be quite strange but I had no reason to doubt its veracity. He told me that growing up as a young man in the 1970s he led a criminal life. In the area in which he was living a young lady died. Just before her burial the girl came back to life. She told the people that she had been given three more days and that she would die again. Meanwhile she would go to three places to tell her story and to encourage the people to "turn from their evil ways."

One of the places she went was where this man was staying. After speaking to the crowd in a hall she asked all of them to shake her hand at the door as she was leaving, as this would be her way to say good-bye to them before she died again. When she came to this man, she looked at him and said, "I know you did not believe what I was talking about. I cannot force you to believe. All I want is a promise from you that the next time you hear someone preach you will surrender your life."

The girl died, the next day as she had said. The man "surrendered" his life after three months. Soon after, he went to a solitary place to pray. During prayer, he saw the girl in a vision thanking him for honoring his promise and encouraging him to stand by his decision. He says the girl appears to him from time to time, especially, in times of crisis and moments requiring big decisions, providing him with words of wisdom and guidance. For reasons I can't understand, I believe God uses the image of the girl as a guardian angel to this man in his role as a spiritual leader.

Spiritual evolution

The model presented above is not so clear-cut and distinct in real life, as real life is more complex. Characteristics of the different stages intermix and interplay. It is the dominant characteristics that determine the spiritual stage one is in. The stage one is in is their stage of spiritual consciousness. They have reached equilibrium and are spiritually settled. One of the deepest questions for human beings is the search for meaning. Each stage provides an answer to the meaning of life. When the meaning becomes unsatisfactory the individual is forced to explore more.

In the spiritually unconscious stage, the individual is the center of the universe. The only world that exists is the physical and mental world. There is no spiritual world and there is no spiritual meaning. I remember a friend who was asked to say grace before a meal. He thanked the farmers who produced the food on their farms. I said to him, it was good to thank the farmers but maybe it was also good to thank the source of grace that gave the farmers the good health and strength to be able to work on the farms. And that source of grace is a power higher than any human being. Human beings can postpone but cannot prevent death from happening to them. They can modify but they cannot create life, for example. Human beings are immensely powerful, but their power is limited. When an individual begins to contemplate the vastness of life in terms of the years the earth has existed, the vastness of the universe with the earth as just one of the planets, the possible existence of several other universes, and the fact that he or she is just one of seven billion individuals on the planet, the idea that man is the center of the universe begins to lose appeal. *The stream cannot rise above its source.* Surely there must be a hub to which every human being and everything else is connected. As Napoleon Bonaparte put it, "If God did not exist, it would be necessary to create Him." It is the search of this hub that creates a crisis in the individual. The crisis may lead the individual in one of two directions.

The individual may find the explanations he or she is seeking in the humanistic view that puts all belief in human reasoning, or in a view that puts faith in the divine. If he is not convinced with the humanistic view he will find explanation in religion. If he finds explanations in the secular humanistic view, he may close his spiritual search and get settled. If he finds explanations in religion, he will abandon his worldview and open up to a possibility of a spiritual world. This knowledge, however, is usually at the mental rather than at the spiritual level.

For people on the journey of spiritual development, often religion does not satisfy them for long. The greatest weakness of religion for most people is that most of the time it does not provide the individual with a conscious person-to-Person or the I-Thou relationship. Religion tends to emphasize a God who is located in heaven rather than the God who is located within the individual. Religion tends to emphasize a God who is locked in the scriptures—who spoke his words in the past. While the words may provide general principles and guidance, religion in general fails to create a relationship of personal spiritual communication or connection. In short, religion fails to touch the spirit of the individual. Most religious people are able to locate and identify their bodies and minds. But when they come to locating and identifying their spirit, they become blank. They are body conscious and mind conscious but not spirit conscious. A simple test to know whether or not you are spiritually conscious is to see if you can identify and locate your spirit. If you cannot, chances are that your spiritual knowledge is mostly religious.

Religion in general fails to bring the individual to the developmental stage of spiritual consciousness. This is the frustration of thinking people who are pursuing the journey of self-development. When they begin facing these frustrations, they feel "stuck" in religion, and this creates a crisis.

The crisis can lead them in two directions. They may decide to keep on in their religion but not primarily for spiritual reasons. Many people are in religions because they were born there and they want to preserve family tradition. Others join or remain in a religion because they want to achieve a social equilibrium or to "fit in." A religion may also help an individual to deal with fears, insecurities, and issues of the afterlife. Religion may give answers to big issues of life, such as to a mother who loses her only beloved child. Religion may tell her, "The Lord has taken the child home and she is safe in His hands." Religion may also provide acceptability in some societies.

The other direction is to move further on in the journey of spiritual discovery. The people who break through religious confinement to bring about a more meaningful and relevant spirituality are almost always labeled controversial, and opposition almost always comes from organized religion. People in stage one or the spiritually unconscious cannot understand this type of conflict, as they label them all under the religious label.

The challenge with the thinking seeker is that he may be mistaken to think that by breaking through religion, he has also broken through his need for spirituality, which he thought he would find in religion. "If it is not in religion then may be it does not exist," he may think. He may put man again at the center of his universe and human intellect may become his god. But in times of contemplation, he still gets overwhelmed by the vastness of life and the small spot he fills in the big picture. It is this feeling that creates a longing and a search for meaning that cannot be completely annihilated or obliterated. It is also this experience that strengthens the belief that the center of the universe that holds everything together must be a bigger intelligence.

The contemplative thinker may move to the ultimate stage of spiritual development— the spiritual change agent. At this stage, the person has shifted to become a spiritual person. The greatest question at this stage for the thinking person becomes—what is the meaning of my spirituality beyond my personal life? What are my responsibilities to my neighbor? How does my spirituality relate with my professional life? Who am I ultimately responsible to? This lifts one's work from a mere job to a calling with a realization that if there is a calling, there must also be a caller. The individual begins seeing himself or herself as a steward. It is this change that creates spiritual change agents. Once people establish their life trajectory as spiritual change agents, helping angels will be lined up to support them and distracting forces will also line themselves up to sidetrack them. Such a life will be one of decisions and actions in favor of good over evil; such a life will rarely be neutral.

Consciousness

Since development is a natural process, the journey of spiritual development is also a natural process. What determines the speed is the level of consciousness and opening to learning and development by the individual. More consciousness means more choice. When people become conscious of the stage of spiritual development in which they are, they can choose to stay there or move forward.

What can be said about individuals who are seemingly at lower stages of spiritual development, but who have made significant contributions to humanity that can only be associated with the "spiritual change agent" stage of spiritual development? The first answer is "judge not." One may not be able, nor is it always necessary, to determine another person's level of spirituality. Secondly, just because one does not conceptualize spirituality or speak about it the way we do does not mean that they are not spiritual. And for all of us, *if God were not forgiving, heaven would be empty.*

Finally, in the grand design of things, everyone who is working toward the good of humanity is in ally with the grand purpose or the spiritual purpose. These people are part of the great cause, and therefore they may become channels of spiritual power whether or not they acknowledge the source of that power. Spiritual consciousness, however, would give them more choice and power.

The work of spiritual change agents would more appropriately be referred to as a calling—what one is called to do. This implies a relationship, because if there is a calling, there must be a caller; someone must do the calling. The caller may be consciously known or not; whether they believe in Him or not.

Conclusion

The spiritually unconscious are unaware of the existence of the spiritual realm. The religious have a mental assent but not an experiential understanding of the spiritual. Seekers doubt its existence. The personally spiritually conscious experience its reality. Spiritual change agents live in both the physical and spiritual worlds and they have first-hand experience in engaging with forces of good and evil in their effort to shape the destiny of the world. The ability to facilitate deeper and more effective change in an individual or an organization depends so much on the change agent's level of spiritual consciousness. People cannot lead others further than they have gone themselves.

CHAPTER 7: ATTAINING BALANCE

Introduction

Balancing faith and reason requires the ability to work with polarities. Difference does not always mean opposite. A person must be centered and work with the polarity that the situation at hand calls for. This is the essence of situational leadership. A polarity is an apparent paradox. In simplistic thinking, one would side with one side of the polarity and reject the other. One would say, I am democratic in my approach and I would never practice autocracy. In contrast in, developmental thinking, one will side with and work with the polarity that the situation at hand calls for. His or her determining factor for choice of the polarity is the end being sought if the end is an ethical one and also if the polarity employed is an ethical one.

One of the examples I like giving my fellow African young men is the paradoxes that emerge when a marriage relationship is evolving over years.

The first 10 years in a marriage are the most uncertain. Most men think they can get somebody better. They are always wondering if this is the best choice they could ever make. It is only after 10 years, and some people say 20 years, that most men begin thinking "the devil you know is better than the angel you don't know," or the wife I know is better than a girl I do not know or whose motives of coming to me am not sure about. It takes time for most men to harmonize their illusions with realities in this matter. Men may spend many years chasing rainbows. This seems to be part of men's nature. The boy in them never seems to want to grow up. At a deep level, the attraction to young ladies seems to be a deep psychological need of the (naughty) boy (the husband) to run away from the mother (the wife). Husbands are "children" because this does not appear to be the case among most women who are happily married.

Men are naturally hunters. Meaning comes from a sense of conquest. A boy's/man's first conquest is the young wife he marries. Once married, he discovers that he has extra energy that the wife cannot absorb. By nature, this energy is supposed to be invested in his life purpose. The purpose takes away all of the (extra) energy in the man. Investing his energy in his life purpose, in the wife and the children later on, keeps the man balanced and focused. A man without a sense of purpose and strategic convictions is easily distracted. When the life purpose is missing, intuitively most men will seek some other woman or women to invest their energy in. Some will resort to excessive drinking. Usually they will not recognize that this is just an illusion. What they are looking for, they cannot get in the woman, but finding a purpose would give them meaning and satisfaction. When a man does not have a purpose, his energy may become destructive.

Many young people confuse "feeling" and "love." Love is a choice you make and the feeling will follow. It is possible to love somebody without having emotions for them (but the emotions will surely follow). It is also possible to have strong emotions for someone without having love for them. Men are weak on following "emotions" rather than sticking with "love." In most marriages, it is not possible to have the same intensity of emotion for the woman that one had when one fell in love. Emotions take a lot of energy and they play a role at different stages of the marriage relationship. At the beginning all of the energy goes to the emotions with the aim of laying a strong foundation of the relationship and bonding of the couple. When this is achieved, the energy must be distributed to other important issues like children, work, planning for the future, in-laws etc. Most men hate the passing away of the emotional stage in their relationship and keep looking for a new "hot girl" to give them the "feeling."

Many men confuse "beauty" and being "young." There is a natural tendency in a man to be attracted to a young lady. But being young is not the same as beauty. Many young people have left their wives to marry a young woman only to be disappointed after five years to discover that the young girl looks just like or is less beautiful than the wife. True love must be based on connection at the physical, mental, and spiritual levels. This is so deep that passing years cannot destroy. Physical appearance will change, but the person, the mental, and the spiritual will never change.

A friend told me that he met a girl who turned his head. The problem was that he was already married. The only thing that stopped him from making the serious mistake of leaving his wife was the thought of his two children. How can I allow my two daughters to be raised by another man while I am still alive, if my wife decides to get married again?

What young men are looking for in the other woman is not necessarily sex; they just need ways to reproduce themselves: identity (who am I and am I important?) and meaning (what is the meaning of my life?). The answers to these questions can only be found in purpose. No woman, wife or otherwise, can substitute for these.

Young men need to realize that the major driving force that takes them away from their homes is selfishness. It is an illusion that happiness and meaning are somewhere outside, or in some other woman. The truth of the matter is that happiness and meaning are within oneself. The things they are running away from, they will also find where they are running to, because the problem is inside them and not outside. The real reasons you fell in love with your wife have not changed. She is the same beautiful woman you fell for. What has changed is that you have failed to "develop" as a matured man—to identify a worthy purpose that takes all of your attention and energy, and that would give you the right perspective about your wife as a partner in turning your life purpose into reality. The problem is not with the wife. The solution is not with the other girl. The problem is lack of a life purpose and the solution is in finding one.

In protecting a marriage from such unfortunate incidents, the wife has some responsibilities. These include:

1. Helping the husband overcome *low self-esteem*. It is low self-esteem that drives a man to get a younger and sometimes more beautiful girl to "boost his value" in his own eyes and those of his friends. The wife must wisely assure the man that just as he got her, he can get any girl

no matter how beautiful. He has what it takes, he is handsome enough. He does not need any woman or even herself to prove the point. In other words, getting a woman no matter how beautiful is not an achievement that he will be remembered for or be proud of as a true man. His self-esteem must come from within—from within himself.

2. Lovingly encouraging and challenging the man to identify his life purpose and give him all the support she can on his journey of searching for and working out his life purpose. Ask him what is he living for, how he wants to be remembered, what is going to change in the community, country, or in his company for the fact that he existed there? In a tender, wise, and delicate way, keep the husband focused on these questions and render him all the love, support, and affirmations he needs as he staggers along on this journey into mature manhood.

A key lesson for young men is to be found in the proverb, *a wise man marries the woman he loves, a wiser man loves the woman he marries*. Since men are always searching for the illusion of the "new and different," a key lesson for young wives is, *always keep "something" covered or you will become like a sister to him.* This is another way of saying familiarity breeds contempt. Keep the curiosity of the man alive all the time. Do not demystify your womanhood and yourself. Keep the husband on his toes all the time.

Polarities

Working with polarities means working with paradoxes. It also means acknowledging that particular approaches may not work in all situations. Working with polarities means acknowledging that it is important to detach oneself from one's dominant approaches and styles. This enables flexibility in handling any situation that may arise.

Working with polarities also implies becoming conscious of one's natural tendencies and reflecting on how these match the demands of the environment one finds oneself in. For example, if an individual's natural tendency of leadership is a democratic approach but she finds herself working in an organization of people who are not responsible, she may need to shift toward a more autocratic style of leadership.

Individuals usually create comfort zones in their natural tendencies. This makes required shifts difficult. It is like trying to use your left hand when you normally use your right hand.

Dealing with polarities requires being "consciously centered." This means the individual has to learn how to work with opposing tensions. Polarities one has to deal with may include:

- dealing with "one's internal marriage"—one's male and female aspects
- dealing with the adult and the child within oneself
- supporting and confronting
- grounding and focusing
- giving meaning and energizing; and
- reason and faith

Dealing with one's internal marriage

Men and women are fundamentally different in some aspects. But in every human being there are elements or degrees of male and female. *Life has two legs: male and female.* It is how people manage these that enables them to reach a sense of balance in dealing with others—both men and women.

Men are perceived to be "harder" while women are perceived to be "soft." Men tend to be moved more by reason while women tend to be moved more by emotions. This is one of the reasons accounting for the fact that women tend to be more religious than men. Men tend to work more with facts while women tend to work more with feelings. Men tend to be more individualistic while women tend to be more collective. Women tend to have more capacity in handling several activities at once while men tend to concentrate one specific activity at a given time. Women tend to be indirect in communication depending more on body language while men tend to be direct, relying more on the direct meaning of words.

At a glance, men and women would appear to be polar opposites. But to be effective in the modern world, both men and women need both the male and female characteristics and they need to use these as the situation may require. Male leaders for, example will be more effective if they can demonstrate some of the female characteristics as the situation demands, especially when dealing with women. Female leaders would become more effective by demonstrating male characteristics if the situation so requires when they are dealing with men. A person who takes a purely male or female orientation will usually fail.

Dealing with the adult and child within

Both the child and the adult are important. *Ask for advice of the old and go to war with the young.* In every adult there is a child. When we grow up, the child does not disappear, but just becomes less conscious. It is the child who connects when we are relating to children. Children will like somebody who is like them. Children shun anyone who approaches them purely as an adult. Learning to embrace the world of the adult but not throwing away the world of the child is a key developmental requirement.

The adult wants to be independent and in charge. The child is dependent. Both independence and dependence are appropriate in their rightful places. Life is so big there are many things one cannot and does not know. It is the child that helps one to be open to learning and development. It is the child who loves the fact that you do not know everything and therefore should be humble enough to keep on learning. Being a child in this sense does not mean being naïve and gullible. It simply means accepting our full humanity. In fact, it means accepting one of the most important attributes of self-development—humility: the ability to know one's power and its limits, the courage to have faith in what one may not fully understand, and the ability to simplify one's life. This is not a return to dependence, but a shift to a higher level of consciousness. *The child who washes his hands will eat with kings.*

Supporting and confronting

This means supporting oneself when you are doing your work well, and confronting oneself when you are not doing well. It also means the ability and willingness to support others and to confront them as the situation requires. This is the essence of the proverb *if two wise men agree on everything then there is no need for one of them.*

Rising above one's emotions to give a rational response is a key requirement in self-development. This does not mean suppressing one's emotions. It simply means the intended outcome rather than the feeling determines whether one will need to support or confront.

People with an autocratic tendency will find it easy to confront others, while those with a democratic tendency will find it easy to support. Building capacity to transcend one's comfort zone and be flexible enough to employ the polarity required at the time is a key requirement. A key challenge for many people is being stuck in their comfort zone.

The important thing is to be centered. In secondary school, we had a very confrontational headmaster. Students were afraid of him. Whenever and wherever they saw him they literally ran away, even though they had done nothing wrong. I remember a day when he chased me for a distance of about 500 meters because I had forgotten to tuck in my shirt. I was safe only because I crossed the road and by the time he wanted to cross, the traffic light turned red and vehicles started to pass.

During one morning assembly it was announced that he was being transferred, and the whole school rose up in jubilation and celebration for his good riddance. He was replaced by another headmaster, who took the school to the extreme opposite end of the pendulum. He was "too good." Discipline broke down and chaos ensued. There was no authority at the school. When the teachers confronted him, he overreacted by swinging yet to the other end of the pendulum, becoming worse than the headmaster he had replaced. A few months later he met the same fate of his predecessor—a celebration for his good riddance.

Effectiveness can be achieved by generally adopting a middle way. One can only go to extremes or to the polarities when a particular situation demands it. After intervening at the polarity, it is wise to come back to the center.

Grounding and focusing

This means managing a balance between learning from the past and creating the future we desire. The proverb *one cannot know where they are going if they do not know where they are coming from* emphasizes this point. If this balance is not properly handled, one can get stuck in the past and become irrelevant for the present and the future. Many people are stuck in the "good old days." One can also become so heavenly minded that they become no earthly good. In other words, they can become stuck in a dream or fantasy land.

People who cannot learn from their past, their experience, or the experience of others are bound to repeat their and other people's mistakes. People who do not have a culture are like people without roots—the best they can do is to imitate other people's culture wholesale. They have no identity of their own. They imitate especially the identity of the people they admire. In a globalized world, "small cultures" are becoming extinct, leaving their young people hanging in the air resulting in unhealthy levels of imitation and loss of cultural diversity. A European friend told me that his biggest disappointment when he comes to Africa is that he hears the same music on radio stations and TV that he hears and sees back home. The food in the hotels is also just the same. And he said he also sees that young people prefer to speak to each other in English, Portuguese, or French rather than in their own languages. It is predicted that in the next 20 years Africa may become the first continent to be completely alienated from its cultural roots. In fact this is already happening. I remember talking to a grandmother in Mozambique who lamented that she is completely disconnected from her children and grandchildren because they cannot speak their vernacular language. They know only Portuguese and speaking vernacular languages is seen as lack of sophistication and a symbol of backwardness. She lamented that as her generation is dying off so are local languages. She was very emotional and happy to speak with me for more than two hours in her local language and could not believe that young men like me who speak the local language and are proud about it still exist. As I was going back to my home country, she asked me to leave her my cell phone number so that we can talk from time to time as she has found a "speaking partner" with whom she could converse in her own language.

The "self-determination movement" with its emphasis on "creating your future" has been the great force that has brought the world to its current state of development. It is absolutely important. However, when taken too far by an individual, it may create unnecessary frustration. It may also create the arrogance that results from the idea that man is the center of the universe. Self-determination works, especially when it is aligned to the Great Cause. It works when the individual is consciously or unconsciously aligned to the Great Cause—the totality of all efforts aimed at improving humanity.

The challenge is to be able to learn from the past but not to get stuck in it. It is also to be able to "create the future we want" but at the same time to be able to acknowledge that we may not have the final say. It is important, therefore, to *move like the chameleon—looking in front and watching behind.*

Giving meaning and energizing

This means balancing the need to exert ourselves to make things happen, and accepting our limitations—and working with them and not against them. It is not possible to seize all opportunities we come across. It is important to recognize that *there are many good things in life, but they are not all meant for us.* It is also important to recognize that of the challenges that come our way, some will be within our circle of capacity to solve while others will not. It is our responsibility to solve only those problems within our ability to solve. It is also our responsibility to be humble to acknowledge that we cannot solve problems that we do not have the capacity for. *We cannot be Atlas carrying the whole world on his shoulders.*

Many times, people in leadership have the illusion of being invincible. They have problems dealing with the polarity of giving meaning and energizing. They tend to get stuck in the energizing polarity, believing that they have the capacity to solve any problem they encounter. They see themselves as Atlas carrying the whole world on his shoulders. Many times, this comes out of pride, which results in a failure to face issues squarely and to be humble enough to say: "I don't know the answer. I am stepping down to give room to other people more capable than myself to take this organization or country forward." If one creates big problems, it is unlikely that they will be the same individual to solve the problems.

The challenge is to avoid expending the energy that could have been directed more appropriately elsewhere. It is also not to give up at the slightest opposition and thereby miss great opportunities.

Reason and faith

This means striking a balance between dependence or reason and faith in addressing issues and situations. Some people see all problems as requiring a reason only solution. Some may see faith as applying to all problems. *Some people see a demon to be exorcised in every situation.* Balanced people will be open to multiple realities. What is the nature of the issue? Is it one that reason alone can adequately address? Is it one that is beyond reason, and therefore may also require some faith? Can a combination of reason and faith create some synergy? If you have malaria, please take quinine or some other malaria drug. If you have cancer, get the best medical attention you can get—and yes, also go to God. As Zacharias (1994: 118) observes, "From individual need to international struggles, the only hope that makes sense and is legitimate is the hope that comes from God, the hope for life and beyond death. Where there is no answer for death, hopelessness inevitably invades life."

Just as there are faith fanatics, there are also reason fanatics. Most professionals being at the seeker stage of spirituality tend to get stuck in the reason polarity. The faith polarity requires a higher consciousness and maturity. This is why many individuals discover faith in old age or toward the end of their lives.

The faith polarity at the organizational level is more complicated because there are no agreed procedures on how to create space for faith or spirituality in most organizations. Until such a time that organizations learn how to create such space, we may continue to be stuck in the reason polarity, even in situations that call for a faith response or even a combination of reason and faith. Individuals in organizations, especially leaders, need spirituality because they will meet situations and interventions that are beyond physical and mental solutions.

The shadow of blessings

Managing polarities also teaches us that all blessings are also potential curses. A very beautiful girl may have to deal with more temptations, for example. Countries most endowed with precious minerals and resources are also the one most afflicted with conflict and violence.

In his 1997 book, *The Road Less Traveled and Beyond,* M. Scott Peck quotes Lundry, who wrote:

> ...that among the great geniuses of our times, all showed a readiness to discard prevalent views, an irreverence toward established authority, a strong capacity for solitude and a 'psychological unease,' which could cause mental trouble such as depression, anxiety or alcoholism. But if these qualities were not too incapacitating, they actually contributed to the individual's ability to achieve significant creativity, blaze new trails, purpose, radical solutions and new schools of thought.

The point is that an individual must be aware that developing a competence or being gifted with one will also create its shadow. If one does not bring the shadow to consciousness, the competence or gift may not only contribute to one's effectiveness, but also to their ruin. *Those whom the gods want to kill spiritually first they make rich.* Today, we have a lot of talented people and celebrities who have brought themselves to ruin because they did not handle their talents and the success the talents brought them well. Divorce rates, for example, are highest among such people because they may fail to balance the marriage and work polarity well. Cases of drug abuse are also high because they may not manage issues of personal internal balance or equilibrium well. Just managing the public image can be very stressful because there are such high expectations of them by the public. A warning to individual seeking success without balancing it with self-development can be found in the proverb *be very careful what you pray for, God may answer your prayer.*

Being connected with one's self
Being centered also means being connected to one's self and identity. I visited a friend in Mozambique. His mother was staying together with his immediate family in the compound. She was very surprised that I could speak and understand her vernacular language. She explained to me that she felt a very strong feeling of disconnection with her children and grand children because they do not understand, cannot speak and are not willing to learn the vernacular language. They only speak Portuguese and are proud about it. Speaking local languages is seen as being inferior and backward. The woman said she was very worried because as the older generation is dying off so are the local languages. *The death of an elderly person is like burning an entire library.*

She explained to me that there is something about being able to speak and communicate in ones vernacular languages especially when children and young people are talking to elders. There is a sense of deep communication and identity. There is also a sense of continuity of a people including the dead, the living and the yet unborn. In the aspect of language, Africans have been too generous to the English, French and Portuguese with the consequences: *Extensive generosity can ruin a person* and *Mucuna's house was ruined by the foreigner.*

Conclusion

The essence of spirituality is consciousness. It is the awakening of consciousness. With increasing consciousness comes increasing power of choice. Handling polarities requires increasing power of choice. It is when one has power of choice that they can be centered. When they are centered they can go to any polarity that needs attention at the moment, intervene, and come back to the center. Without this consciousness, one cannot be centered. They get stuck in their comfort zone, which may not be relevant in all the situations they may encounter.

CDRA (2003: 22) summarizes the importance of balance in practice when they observe that the pith of developmental practice lies in helping the system to find its balance so that it can continue to emerge. In this sense, balance means mediation between order and chaos, between established pattern and new impulse, between center and periphery. Managing the different polarities without losing the sense of being centered is key for being balanced, which is synonymous with being conscious and aware in helping individuals and organizations or the ability to be present, notice, make meaning and interpret observations, feelings and processes.

The preacher expounds the concept of polarities when he states that there is an appointed time for every event under heaven:

A time to give birth and a time to die; a time to plant, and a time to pluck up that which is planted;
A time to kill, and a time to heal; a time to break down, and a time to build up;
A time to weep, and a time to laugh; a time to mourn, and a time to dance;
A time to cast away stones, and a time to gather stones together; a time to embrace, and a time to refrain from embracing;
A time to get, and a time to lose; a time to keep and a time to cast away;
A time to rend, and a time to sew; a time to keep silence, and a time to speak;
A time to love, and a time to hate; a time for war and a time for peace.

Ecclesiastes 3: 1 – 8

CHAPTER 8: SPIRITUAL PRACTICES AND DISCIPLINES

Introduction

Developing spiritual insight to enable individuals and organizations to identify, surface, and confront their contradictions or shadows for deeper and more sustainable change requires the cultivation of some spiritual practices and disciplines. Just as the body and mind need to be fed, the spirit, too, needs to be fed. It needs to be cultivated and nurtured to ensure its health and growth. Proper nurturing of the spirit depends on understanding its threesome nature: the conscience, intuition, and communication or fellowship. Based on this, spiritual practices and disciplines involve two main activities. These are listening to one's conscience, and developing one's spiritual communication. These become one's habits as excellence comes from habit and not from sporadic or haphazard activities.

Crafting a personal vision

Spirituality from a developmental point of view is understood within the context of personal mastery or self-development. For a long time, self-development efforts have not been conscious about the spirit or about how to develop it. They have mostly concentrated on the development of the mind. The value that spirituality brings to self-development is the conscious attention it brings to the development of the spirit.

Real personal vision or a sense of mission comes from much deeper than the mind. People driven by a sense of mission testify that their sense of vision or mission came from a deeper dimension. And that it came instantly or gradually as a revelation or as an unfolding from the intuition or from the spirit.

I describe my own personal experience as an "evolution of consciousnesses." After two years of training, I started practicing as an organizational development practitioner under the mentorship of a more experienced practitioner. The challenge I faced immediately was how to surmount the communication problem we faced. Most of the organizational development models and concepts are developed in Europe and America. They have limited application in other contexts like in Africa.

Communicating them effectively in rural African communities was a huge hurdle. After a long period of reflection, it suddenly dawned on me that the answer was right under my nose. My mentor had been experimenting with using African proverbs as a tool for contextualizing the language of organizational development. I saw sense in what he was trying to do, and with him being British, I also saw his limitations in the endeavor. I talked with him, and we agreed that I could take over this assignment. Like a stroke of magic, the first paper I wrote with him for publication on how to use African proverbs as a tool for organizational capacity building became quite a success. I went ahead to write my first book, *Understanding Organizational Sustainability through African Proverbs*. The response from the book sealed my strategic conviction that my life contribution as a professional will be to promote African indigenous wisdom (African proverbs, folktales and concepts) as a tool for development in general and organizational development in particular. The evolution of this vision was not a very rational process. It was mostly intuitive.

It requires spiritual power to appropriate and stand for a vision, especially if it is not in the mainstream of society and also in challenging situations where jobs are primarily about a livelihood as compared to making a contribution to society.

Crafting a vision is relatively easy; what is more difficult is to reconcile the difference between the vision and the current reality or to bridge the gap between the two. In other words, how to turn the vision into reality or the actual implementation of the vision. In a way, the vision is spiritual in the sense that it is in the realm of faith—not yet manifested in the physical reality. The current physical reality may be and usually is the opposite of one's vision. The gap between the two may seem impossible to bridge, and yet it is this gap that inspires faith for action. As long as people keep their eyes fixed on the vision, they will keep moving toward it by faith. If they keep their eyes fixed on the current reality, doubt or negative faith will keep pulling them or will keep them stuck in the current reality. The battle between faith and doubt are the realities of an individual on the journey of personal mastery. Faith is taking action to bring the current reality into congruence with one's vision. Doubt is taking action to bring one's vision down to the level of one's current reality. In other words *doubt kills vision.*

Spiritual power is needed to ensure that the goals one is seeking are not eroded through doubt. A true vision is a spiritual power of inspiration to the individual. It is a magnet pulling individuals to their desired future. A true vision has inherent power in itself to infuse the individual with perseverance and patience.

It is the spirit that enables an individual to deal with complexity. People who can locate and identify their spirit express higher levels of personal mastery. Peter Senge (1990) quotes Inamori Kazuo, who says: "When I am concentrating....I enter the subconscious mind. It is said that human beings possess both a conscious and a subconscious mind and our subconscious mind has a capacity that is larger by a factor of 10."

What psychologists call the subconscious mind is what in spirituality is called the spirit. It is the consciousness of the spirit and how it contributes to personal mastery that may hold the key to or determine the future of the human race.

Consciousness of spirituality or the spirit and its role in personal mastery is what makes integration of intuition (faith) and reason possible. For true effectiveness, reason and faith must work together in a complementary manner. Great ideas often flow from the intuition, and they have to be made explicable by the reasoning mind.

A vision, being spiritual in nature, always drives one to commit to something larger than oneself, becoming a force of nature in the process. The drive is always the desire to serve mankind. The bigger the vision one is pursuing the more the power that will be channeled through them. Peter Senge further quotes Inamori, who states: "I do not believe there has been a single person who has made a worthwhile discovery or invention who has not experienced a spiritual power."

Cultivating spirituality

Integrating spirituality is about cultivating spiritual virtues. According to James (2011: 94), these virtues include:

Humility—depending on divine power to value others' contributions, to genuinely listen, being honest with oneself, owning one's weaknesses and being a lifelong learner.

Compassion—for the people in one's life especially those one is working with as clients, not being ignorant of their weaknesses, but being merciful. This also includes overcoming adverse reactions to others' bad behaviors and earnestly desiring the best for them—giving them hope and faith that they can change.

Patience—accommodating others with a different pace and standards; and appreciating that processes take time.

Determination—producing work of the highest standards and following through with utmost rigor.

Generosity—in one's relationships and in one's approach.

Self-control—being a careful steward of one's time and resources.

Honesty—being true to oneself and others and ensuring grace and truth in all dealings.

These are very high ideals by human standards, making reliance on divine power a necessity. Spiritual fitness requires humility and reliance on divine help.

Developing these virtues is done through working with one's spirit—the conscience, communication, and intuition.

The conscience gives one a sense of right and wrong. It is the internal guide. When faced with a situation where one is not sure whether something is right or wrong, by silently listening to the conscience one gets the right answers. This is the basis of the statement, *listen to your heart.* Spiritual development requires a deliberate creation of or investment in strengthening one's conscience and in exercising it on matters of choice. It is the conscience, when listened to that gives each one of us a personal "code of conduct" and a sense of principles and values. A measure of spirituality is the ability to listen to and act according to one's conscience. Societal change happens as a result of individuals or groups of people acting on the basis of their conscience. When people of conscience stand up for their convictions there is no way of stopping them.

Developing one's spiritual communication involves using one's faculty of fellowship with the Spirit or God and using one's faculty of intuition to hear the

Spirit's "still small voice." This completes the person-to-Person communication process. The person speaks to the Person through the fellowship faculty, and the Person speaks to the person through the intuition faculty. The ability to "hear" from one's intuition or at least to sense some movement in it is an important indicator of spiritual life. In fact, the most important thing that can be said about personal spirituality is that the spiritual person is able to listen to his or her intuition. The basic limitation of the non-spiritual person is that he or she is not aware of his or her spirit or intuition. It is also important to note at this point that the "inner voice" may be a message from God to guide individuals toward their purpose or a message from Satan meant to distract and mislead them. It is the nature of acts that one is being guided to that determines the origin of the voice. This calls for a strong and more sensitive conscience and the need for "mature" colleagues and advisors. Many people who kill others in the name of God genuinely "hear" the command to do so in their intuition, but the source of such voices cannot be God.

Dr. Joseph Murphy (2006) gives some suggestions on how to get guidance from the intuition. These include:

- Quieting the mind and stilling the body.
- Mobilizing your attention; focusing your thoughts on the solution to the problem at hand.
- Trying to solve the problem with the conscious mind until all considerations are exhausted.
- Thinking about how happy you would be about the perfect solution— sensing the feeling you would have if the perfect solution were yours now.
- Letting your mind play with this mood of happiness.
- Get busy with something else—the answer will most likely pop up in your mind when you are busy working on something else.

Spiritual development involves two main activities: listening to one's conscience, and communication. Spirituality is about a relationship between the human and the divine. The essence of any relationship is communication. Nurture the communication and you nourish the relationship. It will blossom and flourish. Starve the relationship of communication and it will wither and eventually die. The best way to kill a relationship is to stop its communication.

Spiritual development is supposed to be simple, but many times it is made to look very difficult, mysterious, and complex. The disciplines and practices are, also, supposed to be as simple as explained above. Religious people believe in a God who stays in heaven as compared to a God within. They therefore believe that they must perform rigid rituals in order to approach Him. They do this in the belief that *rituals are tributes to the spiritual.* Spiritual people know that God stays within them and they have a conscious and ongoing fellowship with Him. They know that *praising God in the morning is not enough for the evening.* They do not need a special place or time of day to communicate with Him. *The kingdom of Heaven is within you.*

There is no school on earth that teaches people how to pray. They may teach the principles and techniques of prayer, but people learn to pray by praying. Teaching people to pray would be like teaching babies how to communicate with their mothers. When a person gets to the person-to-Person relationship, he or she instinctively learns how to communicate with the Person, and this capacity grows and increases over time and with practice. Though his prayers may be incomprehensible at the beginning, like a mother and her baby, the Person understands him. This is "living" prayer, not written or memorized prayer. This prayer comes from the heart. It is communication in a conscious and living relationship. A key prayer request of the spiritual person is for more wisdom—wisdom in handling relationships with others and wisdom in turning his knowledge into useful practice. *Wisdom is a spiritual bank to the owner.*

A personal case

To implement the disciplines I spend one hour every morning before I start my day. I try to follow this routine as much as I can especially when I am at home. It sometimes gets disrupted when I travel. Guided by the proverbs, *an hour for God and an hour for yourself* and *tune your harp frequently,* I divide the hour into three parts of 20 minutes each. The first 20 minutes is for feeding the conscience. I do this by reading a portion of Scripture and taking time to meditate on it—what is it saying to me? Are there good things I am encouraged to build on? Are there things I should stop doing? Are there some things I should modify? I mostly base my meditation on the life and teachings of Christ as presented in the gospels. He is a model of a spiritual change agent. A conscience that is not fed will become weak and lose its sensitivity. Who has the right of moral leadership to tell others what is right or wrong? After the law of the land, this becomes a personal decision, but following a well-cultivated conscience ensures safety.

The second 20 minutes is further divided into two sessions of 10 minutes each. I spend the first 10 minutes speaking to God. I spend the next 10 minutes quietly listening just in case He also has something to say to me. Does He speak? Yes. I remember a time when a lady friend asked me to help her in prayer as she was making a crucial decision whether to accept a proposal from a man. A few minutes after speaking to God on the matter, I heard a distinct inaudible voice in my heart which I knew was clearly not my own thoughts. The voice said, "That man is not her husband, and neither are you." I was very surprised because I did not say anything in the prayer about myself. I had really not thought about her in those lines although I was not married and I did not have a girlfriend. May be God was taking a preventive measure.

A friend told me of a vivid dream he had one night. In the dream he was told to go to his vegetable garden, which was 15 minutes away. He immediately woke up and went to the garden, where he found a group of five men just about to leave with bags of vegetables that they had just harvested. Frightened by his presence, they dropped the bags and ran away.

I do not speak written prayers. I do not recite memorized prayers. I speak to God like I speak to any person. I do not have any rituals for speaking to God or listening to Him. I just listen quietly, trying to make sure my mind does not wander.

I personally believe that prayer must go beyond "talking to God." It must embrace the whole way of life, making one's life and its conduct become one continuous prayer.

I spend the last 20 minutes thinking and planning the day before me. I also think about the issues I am dealing with in my life at the moment, trying to see them through God's eyes—how does God look at this issue? How can I best go about it with His guidance? I also think about my organizational clients—trying to put myself in their shoes and comparing with what I think to be God's mind on their situation and making decisions on how to proceed. I remember a time when I had to decide whether to go to America to pursue further studies and explore possibilities of settling, or stay at home and support my wife who had just given birth to our first child. Being a young man just out of school it was a big decision to make. I did not have any financial base for my wife if I left, and we had only been married for a year. I mentally detached myself so that I could look at the issue more objectively. During my morning thinking times, a thought began to form in my mind and it grew stronger by the day. The thought was a question: "Where are you needed most?" I finally concluded that I was needed more at home and I let the American opportunity pass me by. I sometimes wonder how my life would have turned out if I had followed that route, but of course there is no way of knowing.

Life is always teaching us something—if we care to listen, observe, and contemplate. *Life is a message, heed it.* I remember a woman, a wife of one of our employees at the organization where I worked as a program manager. She came to my house, which was in the same campus where our offices were, one weekend, and pleaded with me to fire her husband. The husband worked in our accounts department and was also responsible for stores. "Please fire my husband," she insisted. "He is a thief. He steals things from the store and he also steals the organization's money. The house we are building is being built with money and materials he steals from here. I am his wife and I can't tell you lies, so please fire him," she pleaded with me. I was surprised. I had never encountered such an experience before. I told her that *if you see a toad running during day, it means that something is after its life* and asked her what the real issue was. When and I quizzed her further she revealed that the issue about her husband's theft was true, and she wanted to use this to save her marriage. She said he had a girlfriend who stayed somewhere between the office and their home. She had done all she could to stop the affair but to no avail. Her last resort was to get the husband fired so that they could move away from the girlfriend. She hoped her husband would get another job and the other woman would be out of the picture.

The other day I was wakened at three in the morning by the guards. They brought a woman from a neighboring village who was caught trying to sneak out of the hostel at our training center. When I asked her what she was doing there, she said she had spent the night there with one of our drivers. I called for the driver and he confirmed the woman's story. I felt like Christ being quizzed by the people who had caught the woman in adultery. The guards wanted me to "act"—especially against the driver whom apparently they did not like for their own reasons. I was disappointed with the driver, but I did not think it would be wise to punish him harshly as I saw this as his own private issue—though he was not right to bring the woman into the campus especially since it was a religious institution.

I had to do something to show the guards that their effort to apprehend the woman and bring her and the man to me at that early hour of the morning was worthwhile, and I also wanted to protect the driver from what I sensed was their primary goal of reporting the issue to headquarters, which would mean instant dismissal. This was a very difficult polarity to manage. When I went to the office, my deputy—who happened to be a European expatriate—had already heard about the story. She could not agree with my reasoning. To cut a long story short, the matter was reported to headquarters and the driver was immediately dismissed.

The above two examples or polarities are the type of issues I take into my thinking sessions. I ask myself the old Sunday school maxim, "What would Jesus do?" This process helps one to develop a spiritual perspective on very complex and sensitive issues. It is also a way of cultivating wisdom in handling delicate matters.

Thinking sessions also offer one an opportunity to rethink one's values and principles in life. Soon after graduating from college, I got a job as a research assistant. The job took me all over the country. During one of my field trips about four hours from home, I stayed with a former classmate. On the day I was preparing to return home, my host came running from his office (he was a teacher at a secondary school and his house was within the campus). He told me that he had just received a phone call notifying him that a student at the college we had attended, who we both knew had been very sick, had just passed away. The person who had called, who I was made to understand was the aunt to the deceased, asked my friend to notify the college officials about the sad news. Apparently she did not have the number of the college. Since I was going in the same direction and had planned to pass by the college to see my girlfriend (who is now my wife), he asked me to notify the college officials on the family's behalf.

When I arrived at the college, I went to the deceased's best friend. He was shocked and began to cry. After spending some time with him, I went to the leader of the students' union who took it up to the administration. The next day the college provided a big bus, which was packed to maximum capacity with students to travel to the home of the deceased student for the funeral ceremony. They were dressed in their traditional funeral clothing.

Meanwhile, I was still at the campus with my girlfriend. In the afternoon, I got the shock of my life—the story of the death of the student was not true. They found him alive and I don't know who was more shocked—the "deceased" student or the visiting students. They had to create a clever story on why they had come.

This one incident made me rethink the role I had played in the whole fiasco, and think about possible changes in the future of similar issues. Was it really my role to bring such news to the college? Could I not have asked his best friend to confirm the news before going to the administration?

Solitude and meditation

Solitude is a prayer. For people at the personally spiritually conscious stage, the above spiritual investment may be adequate. People at the level of spiritual change agents working at a higher scale and level in bringing about developmental change for larger groups of people may need more investment. Clearer thinking is enabled when one arranges for regular periods of solitude. It is during these periods that one can concentrate and indulge one's imagination without distraction. This is because *one can think best when at rest.* Moses spent long hours in solitude. At one time he spent 40 days and 40 nights as part of his mission to take the Israelites from bondage in Egypt to the Promised Land in Canaan. Solitude and meditation create more space in the spiritual change agents' lives to enable more spiritual power to flow through them. To be effective, they often need to balance the polarity of spending time with people and spending time alone in solitude. They need to spend time with people so that they properly connect with them, and they also need to spend time alone so that they can draw spiritual power to be useful and helpful to the people.

It takes faith to appropriate spiritual power. Faith is the hand with which one receives spiritual gifts. Solitude and meditation strengthen and increases one's faith. A key attribute for spiritual change agents is their love for people. They sacrifice so much through solitude and meditation out of their love for people and humanity in general. A person who does not love cannot be entrusted with spiritual power to bring about greater human good. Such a person is likely to abuse the power by applying it to personal interests, hurting himself and others in the process.

A person who is simply looking for a career may not need to make the sacrifice required at the spiritual agent level.

Meditation refers to an intense dwelling in thought upon an idea or a theme, with the aim of thoroughly comprehending it. The idea or theme mediated upon is not only understood, but it also becomes part of oneself or one's character. Meditation is the secret of all spiritual growth, unfolding, and power. It is the silent reaching of the spirit toward the eternal. It is the basis of all spiritual power. Petitionary prayer without meditation is a mere religious ritual and is powerless to lift the spirit to levels of consciousness required for personal and service effectiveness. Meditation is the real spiritual work. It is through meditation that battles are won in private before meeting them in public. It is not possible to win in public after losing in private.

Meditation involves the discipline of choosing some place and time for regular deep thinking. Most spiritual people have the habit of waking up early in the morning. If mornings are not convenient, one can set aside some time in the evening, preferably just before retiring to bed. If this is also not possible, one can use the short time one has throughout the day. Meditation refers to concentrating or holding thoughts about the divine or about the ultimate good. It may mean thinking deeply about oneself in comparison to one's ideal. Meditation may involve trying to understand oneself with the aim of removing all identified errors. This will involve questioning one's motives, thoughts, and acts—comparing them with one's ideal and dealing with the issues arising impartially. Humility means being harder with yourself than you are with others. Meditation may also be based on one's role model or ideal person or persons and thinking through how to pattern one's life after them.

Meditation may mean deeply reflecting on some attributes of God like omnipotence (the unlimited power of God), omniscience (God's all knowing attribute) and omnipresence (His ability to be everywhere at the same time) and asking oneself what this means to me and my relationship with Him. It may also involve consciously patterning one's life after some spiritual role model by focusing on some attributes of an individual one admires, and asking oneself how one may cultivate those attributes in one's own life. It is this process that gives an individual the mental and spiritual equilibrium. Through this process, one gets more and more spiritual power and fortitude to meet any challenge in life. A great person will lose his power and influence if he neglects the practice of meditation.

Just as it is not possible to make strides in life without sacrifice, it is also not possible to make strides spiritually without the sacrifice that meditation demands. If people are really committed to making a contribution toward individual and organizational effectiveness they will be willing to make this investment. A key vice to be conquered is laziness. True spiritual awakening also awakens the mind and the body. Meditation cannot be separated from the discipline of putting the mind and body under control.

Contemplation

Contemplation put simply means deep thinking. It is a way of cultivating one's mind as emphasized by the African proverb *knowledge is like a garden, if it is not cultivated it cannot be harvested.* Meditation and contemplation are the same in essence. The only difference between the two is the nature of the thoughts meditated upon. Meditation is primarily involved with spiritual matters, while contemplation is mostly concerned with one's work or profession. As we cannot separate our spirituality our work, meditation and contemplation are both spiritual disciplines.

Contemplation involves fixing the mind on an idea or thought without wavering. It also involves the discipline to keep getting the mind back when it begins to wander. Contemplation is a process that takes time to master. With consistent use, one's capacity for contemplation becomes stronger and stronger. Contemplation strengthens one's sensitivity to intuition. The questions one reflects on during intuition prompt responses from the intuition. It is important to have a pen and paper handy during contemplation so you can jot down any insights that may come from your intuition. Contemplation enhances one's alertness and creativity while at the same time developing one's powers of concentration. Contemplation enables one to get a level of depth and insight that one may not have even after reading so many books on a subject or a topic.

One may also contemplate on nature based on such proverbs as *treat the earth well, it was not given to you by your parents but was loaned to you by your children.*

John Kehoe (1997: 49) gives some suggestions on how to awaken one's intuition:

Step 1: Spend several minutes reflecting on the fact that you do indeed possess a spirit and that you have access to the spiritual world and spiritual resources through your intuition. Try to get beyond mental assent or mere intellectual understanding of this fact to where it becomes a personal conviction at a conscious level. Contemplating on this enhances one's consciousness of one's spiritual being.

Step 2: Believe that the Spirit is working with your spirit to give you the guidance you need in all aspects of your life. Affirm this fact to yourself several times during your quiet time in the morning or in the evening just before sleeping.

Step 3: Spend deliberate moments of silence with the aim of listening to your intuition. Sometimes there will be a message from the intuition and sometimes there may not be. It will also take some time for the individual to develop the capacity to differentiate between the voice of intuition—the still small voice—and the voice of the conscious mind. The voice of intuition may not come in response to direct questions. Sometimes the messages come unbidden and at unexpected times.

Reading and contemplation go together. Reading leads to learning. Contemplation leads to plucking the fruit from the tree of books and adding nourishment to one's mind and work. Without serious thinking, reading becomes a waste of time. It is important to master the books one reads. It is important to read them thoroughly until one squeezes all of the juice from them, leaving the pith like after chewing sugarcane. This enables the book to sink into one's very self. It is important to take notes as one goes through a book and to analyze the notes in relation to one's purpose and reading needs.

Reading one book thoroughly will affect an individual more deeply than simply perusing many books. Skimming through many books without going into depth only results in little learning and pride. Putting meditation away and replacing it with much reading also results in shallow thinking and unhealthy dependence on theoretical knowledge.

Mandela (2010: 211 – 212) summarizes the importance of solitude, meditation, and contemplation by reflecting on his own prison experience:

Incidentally, you may find that the cell is an ideal place to learn to know yourself, to search realistically and regularly the process of your own mind and feelings. In judging our progress as individuals we tend to concentrate on external factors such as one's social position, influence and popularity, wealth and standard of education. These are of course important in measuring one's success in material matters and are perfectly understandable if many people exert themselves mainly to achieve all these. But internal factors may be even more crucial in assessing ones development as a human being. Honesty, sincerity, simplicity, humility, pure generosity, absence of vanity, readiness to serve others—qualities which are within easy reach of every soul—are the foundations of one's spiritual life. Development in matters of this nature is inconceivable without serious introspection, without knowing yourself, your weaknesses and mistakes...Regular meditation, say about 15 minutes a day before you turn in, can be very fruitful in this regard. You may find it difficult at first to pinpoint the negative features in your life but the tenth attempt may yield rich rewards. Never forget that a saint is a sinner who keeps trying.

Conclusion

The practice of the change agent cannot rise above his or her own level of self-development or consciousness. You cannot give what you do not have. You cannot lead others to where you have not reached yourself. Raising one's level of self-development or spiritual consciousness can be attained through cultivation of the spiritual practices and disciplines. This will provide a private victory before the public victory of enabling individuals/organizations to identify, surface, and confront their contractions or shadows for deeper and lasting change.

The spiritual disciplines and their effects on the individual are as a result of both human and divine initiatives. The disciplines help cultivate the spiritual nature of the individual by placing one's mind, temperament, and body under divine guidance, wisdom, and seeking the grace of divine transformation. The individual's responsibility is to work hard at the disciplines, but at the same time to receive everything he or she is or has by grace (as a gift or unmerited favor from the Spirit). If one fails to appreciate this grace, they may fall into pride, thinking that when they practice these disciplines they are better than those who do not. They may be tempted to reduce spirituality to a set of external practices rather than an internal grace-driven process of transformation (Wilkinson, 1999: 370). Spiritual practices must be seen as external practices that express and reinforce internal aspirations. The focus should be more on the process of inner transformation than on outward routines. Failure to do this will cause one to fall into the same problem of much of religious practice, which may emphasize ritual at the expense of inner transformation.

According to Munroe (2005: 275), cultivation of the human spirit involves nurturing:

- the spirit of resilience—the ability to see failure as a temporary and necessary step to success
- the spirit of courage—the ability to transform one's fear into a motivator for action and change
- the spirit of patience—a belief in the potential of change and the ability to wait for it
- the spirit of compassion—sensitivity to the worth of others

- the spirit of self-value—a belief in one's inherent abilities
- the spirit of perseverance—the ability to never give up or surrender to the context or the situation
- the spirit of strategic thinking—the ability to plan rather than panic
- the spirit of time management—the conscious application of time to goals
- the spirit of higher tolerance for diversity—a belief in the beauty and strength of variety
- the spirit of self-competition—the practice of never comparing oneself to others, but only with what one has been or done before

CHAPTER 9: AFRICAN PROVERBS FOR PERSONAL AND ORGANIZATIONAL EFFECTIVENESS

Introduction
Spirituality is about cultivating wisdom. African proverbs contain deep wisdom and insights that can be used to help individuals and organizations improve their effectiveness. African proverbs offer a rich mine of material for meditation and contemplation. In Africa we believe that *every proverb is a sacred text* and that *proverbs reflect the divine*. This chapter will present some of the proverbs as an illustration on how this can be done.

Direction and focus
How will you be remembered?
You can only jump over a ditch if you have seen it from afar.

Creating a personal sense of vision and mission enables individuals to be intentional about the contribution they want to make and the legacy they want to create and leave behind. It helps one to set one's priorities in order. Maxwell (2008: 248) reports the results of a survey that was conducted with 50 people who were all over the age of 95. They were asked one question: "If you could live your life over again, what would you do differently?" Three main themes consistently emerged from their responses:

- If I had it to do over again, I would reflect more.
- If I had it to do it over again, I would risk more.
- If I had it to do it over again, I would do more things that would live on after I am dead.

These themes provide deep wisdom to those who are at a stage in their lives to put them into practice.

How is your success affecting you?
Those whom the gods want to make poor first they send important visitors.

Success attracts recognition and admirers. While this is good and satisfying, it may also pose a big danger. Handling success is as difficult as creating it. A woman of a very successful local community agriculture development initiative had this to say: "When we became successful, we began to receive visitors one after another. We started getting invitations to national and international conferences. In the process our work suffered. We worked less and less. The other time I came back from an international conference and we found all the pigs dead."

It is important to ensure that the way we handle visitors who come to learn from us and admire our success and how we handle the invitations we get do not harm our personal effectiveness or that of our organization.

Do you know that your organization could be the best for you in the world?
A happy man marries the woman he loves; a happier man loves the woman he marries.

Many people are not satisfied with the organizations they work for. They believe that some other organization out there is better than theirs. Many times they are attracted by the higher remuneration or better benefits offered by the other organizations.

What we see from a distance, however, may not be the full truth about the organizations we admire. Each organization has its own problems and challenges. Each organization has its own light and shadow. Moving to another organization in search for a perfect organization may end with disillusionment.

Instead of running away, we must make efforts to transform our own organization into the organization we want it to be. If we manage to do this, we will be more satisfied than if we had gone to enjoy the freedom that somebody else's intelligence and hard work had created.

Culture and values
How open-minded are you?
Truth is truth irrespective of the source.
It doesn't matter if the cat is black or white as long as it can catch the mouse.

Sometimes our key to break through as an individual or an organization is found in the most unlikely places or with the most unlikely person. Our minds have been conditioned to expect good things from certain places and certain people, and this may close us off from some opportunities.

How open minded are we when we listen to people we do not expect to offer much to us, or when we visit places where we believe we cannot do much business? When seeking ideas in the organization, do we only go to those in senior positions? When junior staff or volunteers bring their ideas, do we accommodate them or pay no attention to them?

It requires conscious effort and humility to open our minds to the possibility that our personal and organizational lives can be forever changed by an idea of a humble "tea-server" in the organization. We need to objectively look at the quality of the ideas and not necessarily the people who offer them.

What drives you?
If money grew on trees, many people would be married to monkeys.

Individuals and organizations need money to survive, grow, and prosper. Profit, however, is not a goal but a product of good management and leadership. Seen from another angle, money is a means toward an end. It is not an end in itself. It is a means toward the accomplishment of the organization's mission.

Many organizations will do anything to get money. Some non-profit organizations will forget their vision to get "easy" donor money that has no relationship whatsoever with their vision or mission. Some businesses will cut corners or use shortcuts to enhance profits.

It is always important to base our actions concerning money on our values and our identity—what we want to be known for. As individuals and organizations, we must identify a core set of shared values, bring them to consciousness and practically live them every day. There must be systems to reinforce the values, and we should not depart from them. Money and profits built on a shared set of values are truly sustainable. We must be driven by our values.

Strategy

What are you basing the assessment of the health of your organization on?
Each new day is the first day of the rest of your life.

If you were perfect yesterday, it does not mean that you are also perfect today. What we were yesterday is not necessarily the same as what we are today. What was adequate for addressing yesterday's problems may not be adequate for solving today's problems.

Every system has a tendency toward entropy or breaking down unless it is maintained and nurtured. Individuals and organizations too, being living systems, have a tendency toward breaking down unless they are maintained and nurtured. Sometimes the most dangerous moments in a person's life is when that person has just been declared "successful"—for from that moment, they may become complacent.

We must have an individual and organizational "check up" each year. This helps us to identify our strengths and weaknesses objectively. Based on the assessment, we can undertake the right action to ensure effectiveness.

What are you clinging to?
Throw away what you don't need.

When carrying out personal or organizational activities, we may form attachments to them. As time goes by, most of the activities we are engaged in become obsolete. As the organization must move into the future, we need to throw away every activity that holds it to its yesterday.

As the environment changes and the needs of the organization, individuals, or clients change, each activity that stops yielding results must be dropped no matter how attractive it is. Our attachment to the activity must not deter our commitment to move forward into the future to which we aspire.

What activities are we currently implementing in the organization or our personal lives? How long have we been implementing these activities? What is the justification for continuing to implement them? Should we abandon some of them?

How thorough are you in your implementation?
A hunter with one arrow does not shoot with a careless aim.

It is important to do one thing and do it thoroughly rather than jumping to too many activities at the same time. The ability to focus and maintain the focus is a strength and a key factor for individual and organizational effectiveness.

Many individuals and organizations are tempted to implement a few more projects because of opportunities in their task environment, while not giving thought to their capacity to deliver. When we do not have the capacity to implement the projects, we are forced to take short cuts. The problem with short cuts is that they damage the quality and impact of the service. Customers and clients will not be impressed. At the end of the day, the individual or the organization suffers.

Reflection and learning
How deep are your solutions?
A bee sting can only be removed by uprooting it.

What we see on the surface as problems are usually just symptoms of deeper underlying problems. If we only deal with the symptoms without addressing the underlying causes the problem will keep coming back in more devastating ways.

A problem of inadequate funding may be solved by writing more funding proposals. A drop in profits may be addressed by strengthening the marketing section of the organization and enhancing the service or product quality. In the case of inadequate funding the root cause of the problem may be a lack of skills and competences in writing high quality proposals or ineffective financial policies, systems and procedures. Unless these deeper problems are addressed, any surface solution will not bring about lasting change.

As individuals and organizations, we need to take time to identify the problems we are experiencing. We need to dig deeper beyond what we see on the surface until we identify the root causes of the problems. We must address our problems at this level for lasting solutions.

When do you celebrate success?
A person who is putting on his armor for war should not boast like the one who is taking it off.
Don't laugh at the fallen ones when you are still standing on slippery grounds.

A truly happy person is the one who has served an organization and is retiring or quitting after realizing personal and organizational goals. Such a person has every reason to celebrate. The right time to boast, therefore, is when we are taking off the armor.

The person who is just putting on armor cannot be completely sure because there are so many slain giants on the battlefield. The best one can do is to take into account all of the factors that are within one's control and do one's best. One should still aim for the sky but the outcome is not entirely under the individual's control.

As we are doing our work, let us hold on until the end so that we can also boast after the successful completion of our contribution to the organization's life. Let us avoid anything that would keep us from a happy ending.

Competition
How well informed are we about the strength of our competition?
It was ignorance that made the rat challenge the cat to a wrestling match.

Many times we get a brilliant idea and we want to immediately rush to the market with it. Before such a rush, it is important to assess the current and potential competition and its strength. It is important to do this by considering such questions as:

- Do we have enough material and monetary resources to sustain the business?
- Do we understand where this service or product will fit in the market?
- Do we have enough capacity to compete favorably on quality and service?

It is always important to be realistic about our capabilities and the realities of the task environment we will be operating in. It is wise to take time to build our capacity before we launch into a market to avoid inevitable failure. We can do this through:

- thinking strategically—challenging assumptions and studying trends and patterns
- creating a long-term vision for the organization
- understanding the strengths of the competition
- identifying and changing organizational core competences like quality, speed, flexibility, expertise, and capacity to innovate

How proactive are you?
The pasture does not go to the cow but it is the cow that goes to the pasture.
There is a saying that "he who waits, waits forever." We all want good things to happen to us but good things will not happen to us. We have to make them happen. We have to go after what we want, rather than waiting for the good things to come to us.

We attract good things into our lives and our organizations by spending our time doing something useful. Enroll in a correspondence course, attend a motivational seminar, read books, seek advice, join a professional club, etc. Make sure your time is spent usefully and productively at all times.

If we do not get what we want in our personal and organizational lives, it is often because we are doing some things wrong or we are not doing enough. Don't just sit there. Do something. When we do something, we will become someone.

Personal mastery
How strongly do you want to succeed?
Determination pays, the sparrow married a pigeon.
Many times we fail to get what we want not because we do not want it but because we do not want it badly enough. Somehow, we have created a comfort zone with our achievements from the past. We mistake wanting to achieve our goal for wishing we had what we want.

As individuals or organizations, we must have a red-hot desire that is all compelling in order to achieve what we truly care about. The desire must be so strong that it literally drives us to the desired goal. It is this type of desire that overcomes every obstacle on the way. Determination starts with creating an inspiring vision of the ideal being sought. After the vision, one must create a challenging goal in each of the major roles one plays in life and set a step-by-step activity plan to achieve the goals along with clear indicators and targets for achievement.

We must also get advice from those who have already walked on similar journeys and succeeded. These are the people who can prove what that they say by their lives and not just by words. Lastly, we must make it a point to be first class in everything we do—to be as good as the best in the world—if not better.

How well are you managing your good times?
Wealth is like a rat's tail, it easily slips away.

Sometimes we find ourselves in an unbelievable situation where we experience no financial limitations at all. As an individual or organization we have all the money we need and more. Such situations, however, usually do not last long. They are temporary. We should therefore not be tempted to think that things will always be like that. When we find ourselves in such a lucky and enviable situation, we must make investment plans that will act as "shock absorbers" to us as individuals or organizations as we move into the unpredictable future.

Extra money for an individual or in an organization is not for wasting. It is for future preparedness. If we squander today's extra money, we may find that tomorrow we have only experienced a short-lived glory. Yesterday's excess may created tomorrow's deficit. Yesterday's millionaires have become today's beggars because of financial mismanagement.

How wide is your scope?
If you live in a small house you may think you have a lot of furniture.

A small house does not have much space. It is therefore easily filled. When we live in a small house we may think we have a lot of property. If we get a chance to move to a big house we are often surprised at how little or few our belongings are.

When our mental scope as individuals and organizations is small, we are often satisfied with our current state of life. When we are satisfied we have no motivation to keep stretching ourselves.

To get inspired to move on, we must stretch our horizons. When we have more "mental space" we will soon discover how little or few our assets really are. It is this dissatisfaction that drives us to seek and become more.

What comes first, your talking or your thinking?
A word spoken cannot be called back.

The wounds caused by words are painful and take longer to heal than physical wounds. For this reason we must always be careful what we say to other people. It is better to say nothing at all than to hurt people with our words.

The times when we are likely to say things that will hurt other people are when we are angry or disappointed. Anger and disappointment cloud our sense of judgment and rationality. When we go ahead and speak in this state, we will usually regret what we said.

When we sense that we are angry or disappointed it is wise to withhold our words and wait until we have cooled down and are more sober. When we are in our normal state, let our words be few but powerful.

Relationships
How are you treating new and young employees in the organization?
You can straighten a tree only when it is young

Young and new employees must be molded into the culture of the organization. This is often a tough process for many, because it may involve a breaking down and remolding process. When we watch movies concerning a trainee and mentor in martial arts, the relationship can teach a lot of lessons. The films usually portray a young, naïve and overconfident young person who is slowly broken down by an elderly mentor and at the same time molded into a more effective individual. It is never an easy process for the trainee, but in the end he or she appreciates the process.

In order to ensure the future survival of the organization, we need young people who are developing and growing to replace us when we leave. These individuals must be at least as good as we are, and preferably better. The only way to ensure this is to create such a crop of people though appropriate and effective monitoring and coaching.

How healthy are our relationships in the organization?
Living close to each other does not mean you are relating well.

Relationship problems cause big strains in organizations. Many organizations do not take conscious efforts to build healthy relationships among the people. This leads to alienation and conflict in organizations.

As long as people are not "fighting" or arguing, leaders may not see it as their duty to encourage and facilitate relationship building in organizations. The best time to build relationships is before they go sour. Prevention is always better than cure.

Relationships must be built among individuals, between departments, and within the entire organization. It is only that which is relating well within itself that can relate well with other organizations and stakeholders.

Organizing social times for the people in the organization and taking regular retreats where people can interact and have fun are some of the ways to encourage and facilitate relationship building in organizations. The more we do these types of things, the better the relationships will become.

In addition, organizations also need proper and effective grievance and conflict-resolution procedures. People must feel that the organization genuinely cares for them and about their grievances.

Leadership development
How courageous are you?
Avoiding a fight is not cowardice.
It is wisdom not to engage in a losing battle. When we have assessed the situation and concluded that our chances of winning are slim, it is wise to pull out of the race. It does not help to go on knowing that we cannot win. When we go into losing battles we waste resources of time, money, and energy. It is bad for morale. The more we lose, the more we doubt our capacities and the more we lose our self-confidence.

We must run only in winnable races. When we do this we build ourselves up. We get more resources. We get more self-confident and we are ready to engage in bigger and bigger fights. We must begin small and grow big over time rather than begin big and be pushed back to where we belong because we were unrealistic or over ambitious.

How much pain do you have in your organization?
Tears never flow in the house of a coward.
A struggle without casualties is not a struggle
Development is a breakthrough to a new level of being, doing, and relating. It is a breakthrough to a new level of existence. Any breakthrough is preceded by a crisis.

A crisis signifies pain. Without pain there can be no development. If all we have in our organizations are good times, chances are we are stuck. If development is happening, we must experience some pain along the way.

Are we avoiding pain in our organization? By avoiding pain, we may be holding the organization from experiencing breakthroughs to new and higher levels of effectiveness. We should not look for pain, but when it comes let us celebrate the development opportunity it will precipitate if we handle it well.

The attitude must be that if we take an approach that is good, it is not by accident that everyone and everything that shows up in our life is there for a reason, and we are moving toward our ultimate destiny for learning, growth, and achievement. We will begin to see every event—no matter how difficult or challenging—as a chance for enrichment and advancement in our life (Canfield, 2007: 75).

How strong are your lenses?
From a distance a lion looks like a baboon.
Many times people do not tell us the truth. We have to establish the truth ourselves. When people offer us deals, they may only show us the good side. They may not show us the full cost we are paying.

When we receive financial and narrative reports, do we read beyond what is contained in the reports? When we want to buy personal and organizational assets, do we apply scrutiny to make sure we are buying the best with the money we have? We should not put too much trust in other people. We should not trust other people more than we trust ourselves. At the end of the day, the final responsibility lies with ourselves. We are the ones to deal with the consequences of our decisions and actions/inactions.

We must develop the capacity for critique. We must also develop the capacity for keen observation. We must always understand that all that glitters is not gold.

How deep is your leadership?
Still waters run deep.

Along the path of growth and development, each individual or organization will meet some crisis. The natural instinct when a crisis hits is to panic. When people panic, they lose objectivity and become powerless.

The real strength of a leader is manifested during times of crisis. Real leaders are invisible until a crisis hits. A leader who runs away, abandoning his people, is not a real leader. While everyone is panicking, the real leader remains calm. He or she is not shaken but rather is strengthened by the crisis. He or she draws from the depth of his or her leadership to calm the storm. Let a crisis hit an organization and you will know who the real leaders are.

Conclusion

In this chapter I have presented some insights from my own experience using African proverbs as material for contemplation. As an organizational development practitioner, I have found that African proverbs contain material for meditation and contemplation as far as personal and organizational effectiveness are concerned. They contain deep insights that can enable individuals and organizations to identify, surface, and confront their contradictions or shadows for deeper and lasting change. A single proverb may produce a deeper insight than an entire contemporary management book.

African proverbs speak much more deeply to individuals and organizations because they communicate at the level of being and relationship. In this sense, they are soulful and facilitative to spiritual growth and development for individuals and organizations.

CHAPTER 10: THE CASE FOR CULTIVATING THE HUMAN SPIRIT

Introduction

The many challenges that individuals, organizations and society as a whole are facing seem to suggest that the idea of saving the world is no longer a practical pursuit. But if by saving the world we mean saving the people, as we believe in Africa, then the only hope for the world lies in cultivating the human spirit. This starts with the consciousness of the reality of the spiritual dimension. It also means going beyond "neutral spirituality" to the conscious reality of good and evil.

Spiritual things are real

In explaining why he is so successful, Aigboje Aig-Imoukhuede, one of Nigeria's most successful bankers, says, "I believe that God's hand is on my life and business. Many things have happened for which there is no explanation except divine intervention" Msafiri (2011: 132). Consciousness of divine intervention is what makes spiritual things real to an individual.

In his book, *Managing the Non-Profit Organization*, Peter Drucker says that any medical doctor who has practiced for at least five years cannot say that miracles or miraculous cures do not happen. If anyone says that, they are lying or they are not being honest. Miracles do happen. The reason miracles are not written about or taught in schools is that we do not know how they happen. There is no body of knowledge that explains how miracles happen. That is why they are miracles. Spiritual things are invisible, but their effects are tangible and can be visible.

The eminent Nigerian prophet T.B. Joshua prophesied about the great fire in England, which happened during the rioting and looting of August 2011. He announced on TV, giving a vivid and detailed description of the event a few weeks before it happened, so that people should pray about it. He also prophesied about the death of the North Korean President Kim Jong-II. In Malawi, the President, Bingu wa Mutharika, died on 5th April, 2012. A few weeks before this death, the same man, T.B. Joshua, had prophesied it with unusual exactness, giving exact details around the time, nature and circumstances of this death. Spiritual or supernatural events do not catch headlines or media attention. BBC, CNN, Sky News, or Al Jazeera could not take this on as news because that is not how they work. Even when the fire actually happened they could not say that it was foreseen, and maybe if action had been taken some damage would have been minimized or prevented altogether. The media, however, will publicize religion and key religious events because they understand religion. It is well documented and they know how it works.

Carl Jung, a key authority figure in the field of psychology, spoke freely on many occasions about his experiences with the supernatural. At one point he talked about an incident in which a large group of ghosts physically and visibly invaded his home in broad daylight and in the presence of his family members

(Hyde & McGuiness, 2005). Such statements coming from a man of Carl Jung's caliber cannot be easily dismissed.

Good and evil

The world is not neutral. Good and evil are realities. Evil is always represented by darkness and good by light. Good is the positive and life-giving power, while evil is the negative and life-constraining power. *Divinity strengthens the soul while evil weakens it.*

Reason alone is incapable of fully explaining good and evil and human responsibility in dealing with these forces. Mentally ignoring evil is not sufficient. It must be a daily practice to rise above it. To mentally affirm good is similarly not adequate—good must, by unswerving endeavor, be entered into and comprehended. Mental assent is not enough. Action is what matters (Jeremy, P. Tarcher, 2010: 25).

Most individuals in high and influential positions have a personal understanding of spiritual pressures they have to deal with in their intention to promote good. Martin Luther King Jr. observed that, "Whenever you set out to build a creative temple, whatever it may be, you must face the fact that there is tension at the heart of the universe between good and evil. This struggle is not only structured out somewhere in the external forces of the universe, it is structured in our own lives. In every one of us there is a war going on" (King, 1998). He calls the war a civil war. Every time we set out to be good, there is something pulling us down, telling us to be evil. Whenever we set out to dream our dreams and to build our temple we must be honest enough to recognize the existence of good and evil.

It is times of crisis and moments of choice that expose the children of light and the children of darkness. In a moment of choice, one cannot be neutral. Being neutral means siding with evil. Spiritually strong people are willing to sacrifice self-interest for a bigger good. Evil flourishes when good men decide to do nothing about fighting evil. The thinking that "I will not do anything about fighting this evil because it is not affecting me directly" is contradictory thinking. *If a lion kills a bad person and it is not killed, next time it will kill a good person, if your neighbor's house is on fire and you do not help him put the fire out the next house to catch the fire will be yours* and *if you are not part of the solution you are part of the problem..* Vigilance must be taken to always put evil at bay.

I remember the level of personal pressure I consistently dealt with when I was working as a program manager in an organization. I was responsible for a training center, which was located away from the headquarters. The center handled huge projects, including construction, and I was responsible for awarding contracts. The construction projects were the biggest. We followed all procedures and awarded the contracts to the most deserving bidders. At night I would often hear a knock at my door from the individuals to whom we had awarded a contract. They would say they had come to thank me for awarding them the contract. They would usually be very surprised when I refused and explained that they deserved the contract and did not need to "thank" anyone.

On my side however, it was not easy. This gave me a tremendous spiritual pressure. I was just beginning my career. I was not married yet. I was 25 years old and seriously in need of money. This made me understand the proverb— *where God boils his yam that is exactly where the devil roasts his fish.* I would reason that getting the money would have given me an equivalent of five years of my salary.

Some people may say that this was only a moral temptation and they may be right. But one thing I remember distinctly about the three years I spent at that work station was the difficult spiritual atmosphere I had to deal with. I have never had a similar experience anywhere else, especially at that level. No matter how much I tried to pray, and occasionally fast, I sensed a "blockage" and could not get a release or breakthrough. Prayer always seemed to be unnaturally hard work. What surprised me also was the paradoxical fact that this place was a "missionary" or religious center. Dr. David Yonggi Cho, pastor of one of the largest churches in the world based in South Korea, says, "When I am in South Korea I pray for two hours per day. When I am in Japan, I pray for five hours because the devil of Japan is stronger than the devil of South Korea."

This is generally an evil world, though a majority of people are generally good—which is a paradox. People generally want to be good and want good things, but evil prevents them from achieving this. This is not the same as the often excuse people give when they are caught doing something wrong and they have no explanation to make apart from, "the devil made me do it." The existence of evil does not take away man's responsibility but rather enhances it. The vivid scenes of 9/11 in America are a clear manifestation of evil that defies reason. And how can the holocaust and genocide in Rwanda be explained apart from the reality of evil? The four tragedies of human depravity: the beggar, the drunkard, the drug addict and the prostitute are clear manifestations of evil.

An example of evil that defied my understanding was a case of a university that was closed simply because of an example a lecturer gave in class. I call the case "the ghost of Egypt." During the Egyptian revolution that ousted Hosni Mubarak in January 2011, a young political science lecturer drew parallels between the factors that led to the revolution in Egypt and the situation in Malawi. Unknown to him, a student in that class who happened to have connections with the police reported him to the power that be. The inspector general of police summoned him for questioning. When he came back he informed his fellow lecturers about the questioning. They were not amused and demanded an apology from the inspector general for infringing on their academic freedom.

Before the inspector general could respond, the President of the Republic, who happened to be the head of both the police and the University as Chancellor of the University, brought himself into the issue. He declared that the inspector general cannot and should not apologize, and for very incomprehensible reasons he said, if the inspector general apologizes it's like it is the President himself who is apologizing. "Have you ever seen a president apologizing to a professor anywhere in the world?" he had asked.

What followed was a protracted stand-off. The lecturers boycotted classes and vowed not to go back to class until their academic freedom was guaranteed. The President vowed not to lose face. The university council, the highest decision-making body in the University, obviously working under influence, went ahead and fired the lecturer and three others who were leading in the protest for "indiscipline." Court battles ensued. Meanwhile, classes came to a halt. The students were caught in the middle. *When elephants fight it is the grass that suffers.*

The university was closed for eight months. It only opened when the President bowed to increasing local and international pressure for him to reinstate the four lecturers he had fired. Eight months of wasted time over no real issue!

What development intervention can address this seemingly irrational crisis? In my opinion this is a naked manifestation of evil. There may be many explanations and therefore different ways of addressing this situation, but the fundamental causes of the case of "the ghost of Egypt" type of scenarios are spiritual.

What makes people who have great power to do good to humanity choose to use that power for bad, if not evil? It is because they have allowed evil to overtake their reasoning. No amount of reasoning can deliver them. A church that bans interracial marriages in the 21st century is just expressing evil. An individual who kills in the name of God is just expressing evil. A person who chooses to remain neutral in a moment of choice between good and evil is expressing evil.

People will always make rational decisions under the circumstances they find themselves in. One may wonder why, when asked by Pilate whether to release Jesus or Barabbas, the murderer, the people chose the murderer? Why did they choose evil over good? Looking at it from the surface may not make sense. It is important to note that wherever there are efforts to bring good, there are always counteracting forces of evil. Jesus was perceived to be bringing a new system that could replace the old system as people would discover its religious weaknesses and hypocrisies. The power base of the leaders was threatened.

In order to preserve and protect their power, many people are ready to use any method possible even if it means employing conscious evil. The people knew that Barabbas was evil. He was a murderer, but they preferred him because he was no threat to their system and power base. They knew Jesus was a good man but they did indeed sacrifice him to preserve and protect their power and system.

Developmental work is mostly concerned with spreading good and therefore, wherever genuine developmental work is happening, it is natural to expect confrontation with people and forces whose self-interest are at risk— whose power base and systems are threatened. We know of journalists who have been tortured and killed for simply doing their work. We know of human rights activists who have been persecuted and killed for standing with the oppressed. Their crime is that they threaten the power base of the oppressor. In his heart, the oppressor knows that these are good people and that they are standing for a good cause, but he would rather employ evil to destroy them in order to protect his self-interest.

Many people cannot sacrifice their self-interest for the sake of promoting a bigger good. This aspect of human nature is part of what sustains evil. It requires high levels of consciousness and power to sacrifice self-interest for the sake of a higher and bigger good.

The ultimate good is personified in a Spirit Person called God. The ultimate evil is personified in a spirit person called Satan. With this understanding, the struggle between good and evil becomes not just a struggle between principles, but between two Persons and two opposing kingdoms with the human mind as the battlefield.

There are some apparent sharp differences between psychology and some religions on the true nature of human beings—whether human beings are basically good or evil or sinful (Collins 1969: 31). The debate is ongoing and shows no sign of abating. My own opinion is that in the holiest person there are elements of evil and in the vilest person there are elements of good. *The pot that cooks food can also cook poison.* Considering the little good that may be in them, labeling other people as bad and avoiding them and their contribution would be the same as *throwing way the baby and keeping the placenta.*

Good people can go bad and bad people can become good depending on the decisions they make and the actions they take. The biblical view of man as being naturally sinful refers mostly to God's requirement for the "salvation of the soul" and not to man's morality. Man is capable of living a moral life without consciously relying on God from the simple observation that it is not only Christians or religious people who live morally upright lives. The biblical emphasis is that morality is not sufficient for man's salvation. The Bible recognizes that human beings are capable of high levels of morality without a conscious relationship with God. An example is the story recorded in Acts 10: 2 about a high-ranking soldier called Cornelius who is described as "a devout man, one that feared God with his entire household, gave much alms to the people and prayed to God always" and yet despite all these moral and religious qualifications, God did not regard him as a saved person. He still needed the Apostle Peter to explain to him how to be saved (to start and maintain a conscious spiritual relationship with God through Christ).

In the sense portrayed above, the difference between faith and reason is just a matter of degree. Reason is a continuation of intuition and conscience, and these are available in varying degrees to every human being. The most unspiritual person depends mostly on logic while the spiritual person depends mostly on intuition, differing only in degree. Every human being has enough reason with which to know and embrace the spiritual if they choose to.

Man is a free moral agent—he can choose whether to be bad or good. And because he has the power to choose, he is responsible for the consequences of his decisions and actions.

Spiritual elements of an organization

According to James (2004), the spiritual elements of an organization include: vision and values, service and love for others, empowering others, relationships of trust, changing from within, courage to overcome fear, and divine energy. Secular humanists may argue that the first six are not necessarily spiritual but their general absence in most organizations suggests that their effective expression may require more than rational human effort.

Vision

Vision and values are seen as the key elements of a spiritually based organization. The importance of vision in an organization cannot be overemphasized because *a good wind has no use to the sailor who does not know the direction.* Organizations are formed to solve a particular problem in society. More positively, they are formed to fill a need or a niche in the world. True vision comes from deeper than the mind. It is intuitive. It comes from the spirit. A true organization is immortal until its purpose has been fulfilled. This immortality comes from the spirit. A true vision is also unique. The uniqueness may be from what the organization is set out to do or how differently it will do what others are already doing while adding distinctive value in the process. Others can imitate the body and the mind of an organization, but they cannot copy its spirit. The spirit is unique.

The true competitive advantage or lever of an organization is its spirit. Cultivation of the organizational spirit is the most effective measure in ensuring its legitimacy, relevance, impact, and sustainability. The organization is strong and truly effective only within the limits of its vision—*the strength of the crocodile is in the water.*

Values

If money grew on trees many people would be married to monkeys—meaning that many people are willing to throw away values for personal gain and self-interest. They are willing to compromise values for personal comfort. It is important to be true to our values irrespective of the various pressures to change and compromise. *Rain falls on a leopard's spots but it does not wash them away.*

Creating a humane organization is one of the biggest challenges facing organizations today. Balancing the efficiency versus effectiveness polarity is one of the most difficult tensions to manage. Sharpening the organization's conscience is a major responsibility for organizational leaders. Visions can be realized only when they are based on strong values that are being adhered to. Whenever we come up with a vision, we create some gaps. One of the gaps is the values gap. Often, there is a need to review the values being practiced to ensure that they are aligned to and congruent with the new vision. The key question becomes what value our vision is demanding of us. In most cases, we cannot realize our vision with the same type of values in our current reality. The conscience is the base of our organizational values. This is what makes values a spiritual matter.

In many organizations, leaders are at a loss as to how to cultivate appropriate values for the organization. It is important to identify the values of an organization in a consultative and participatory manner in order to ensure that they are coming from the collective organizational conscience. What does our vision or mission demand from us in terms of the values we need to espouse? This should be the key guiding question in identifying the values.

It is not enough to identify the values we need. It is also important to differentiate between the people values (what values do we need to work together more effectively within our organization?) and the work values (what values do we need to work more effectively with our customers and clients?). When the people and work values are listed, there is the need, again in a consultative manner, to define what we mean by each value. For example, if we say that one of our values is "team spirit," what exactly do we mean by that? Can we put its meaning in concrete and unmistakable terms? What are the indicators of somebody who is practicing team spirit?

One of the principles of spirituality is "moving beyond knowledge to action." How, then, do we incorporate the values into the organizational system and culture? One of the ways to do this is through the performance appraisal system. Most organizations' performance appraisal systems focus on appraising work-related goals and targets. A few organizations include learning goals and targets. Very few, if any, include appraisal of individuals' adherence to the organization's values.

When it is possible to define the values clearly and concretely with indicators and targets, it becomes possible for individuals and their supervisors to objectively assess their internalization of the values. Entrenching the organizational values would also include "rewarding and punishing" adherence and non-adherence respectively. An organization that is living its values has a strong foundation. It is strong internally and in its work with its clients or customers.

The greatest gift a leader can give to an organization is an inspiring vision. A strong vision can outlive the leader, and in this sense can be a gift to future generations of the organization. The values also provide a strong foundation for the organization's future generations to build on.

A way to make the vision practical is through what Stephen Covey calls a universal mission statement. Such a statement serves leaders of organizations as an expression of their vision and sense of stewardship. The universal mission statement captures, in one brief sentence, the organization's core values, and creates a context that gives meaning, direction, and coherence. It could read like:

To improve the economic well-being and quality of life of all stakeholders (Covey, 1991: 296).

Covey presents five major virtues of the universal mission statement:

- Ecological balance—helps the leaders to think ecologically about all of the stakeholders. By attending to the transforming principles, all stakeholders will enjoy synergistic benefits.

- Short- and long-term perspective—discourages taking the short-term approach and encourages the long-term approach.
- Professional challenge—the few words in the universal mission statement embody enough challenge for leaders throughout their entire professional careers.
- Organizational context—within the parameters of the universal mission statement, leaders can better set policies and procedures, strategy, structure, and systems.
- Personal sense of stewardship—the universal mission statement generates a sense of stewardship with respect to people and other resources.

Creating a spiritual climate in an organization

Embarking on a journey of spirituality is a matter of personal choice—organizations cannot force individuals. The best an organization can do is to provide a supportive environment. Organizations must be able to create "space for grace." They must value both rational and intuitive thinking and give credit to all, when and where it is due.

The essence of spirituality is service. Spirituality is always about transcendence. It flows outwards toward the other. The importance of any internal spiritual experience is determined by observing whether or not the experience a better servant of others. The value of service is paramount in spiritually based organizations. Love is one of the central spirituality concepts. Love and service always go together. The spirit of service is the spirit of love for the client or the customer. And if spirituality is about connection, then service or love becomes indispensable in a spiritually based organization. Making a livelihood is a key and very important motivation for individuals and should be treated as such. But making a contribution through service or love should be a higher motivation. When two organizations are offering the same product or service of the same quality and price, clients or customers will prefer the organization that makes them feel more loved and appreciated. They will go where they feel they are served better. They will go where they can connect with the human spirit in the organization.

Spiritually based organizations emphasize the empowerment of individuals and teams. They encourage them to be free to make decisions, to develop their potential, and to work creatively with others. It is the work of leadership to ensure a climate in which the organization's individual and collective spirit thrives. In some organizations, people with strong spirits and convictions are feared. Instead of ensuring that their energy is channeled positively, they are suppressed. Diversity in thought and views when managed within the framework that is consciously linked to the organization's mission is healthy for the organization, because it encourages innovation and creativity. Independent thinking is accommodated in organizations that believe in empowerment.

Related to empowerment is the issue of trust. In Africa, we believe that the organization one works in is one's second home or family. I remember the challenge I faced trying to convince an American publisher to include this concept in one of my books. "People in America will not understand this," he said. He told me that in America there is a sharp demarcation between work and home. I understood his point, and to a large extent he was right. But I was using the concept of family metaphorically. In a family, one is supposed to feel accepted, loved, and trusted. The weakness of this metaphor, of course, is that in family, issues of performance may not be paramount as they are in organizations.

A key challenge as noted above is how to manage the people and performance tension—how to balance attention to people issues and performance issues. In relative terms, organizations in the industrialized countries are caught up in the performance polarity, while those in the developing countries may be caught up in the people polarity. When there is too much emphasis on performance at the expense of being humane, the human spirit is stifled. When there is too much attention to people, organizational performance suffers.

It is important to emphasize that in managing the efficiency versus effectiveness polarity, trust is paramount. It is also important to emphasize that trust must be earned. In many sectors, including politics and religion, people are generally suspicious about leaders. Leaders have to prove that they are trustworthy—it is no longer taken for granted that they are so. A good number of them, of course, are guilty by association. But they still have to prove that they are different. The way to do this is to demonstrate integrity—where one's words match one's actions.

Trust at the individual level may also mean having the faith that whether or not we feel it, the divine presence is there to help us. Many times, people lose faith when they lose this feeling. One of the greatest fears of a young child is the first day its mother leaves it at kindergarten. He thinks his mother will not come back to pick him up to return home. His concept of trust is tied to physically seeing his mother.

Spiritually based organizations encourage self-knowledge. A key role of the leaders is alignment. A key area requiring alignment is that of aligning individuals' personal visions to the organizational vision. This ensures focus and synergy and a concerted flow of organizational energy. Individuals are encouraged to become more self-aware. *Know thyself* is a key principle and practice in spiritually based organizations. Individuals are encouraged to be aware of their strengths and weaknesses. They are also placed in roles and responsibilities where they can maximize their strengths and minimize their weaknesses. Teams are organized in such a way that the individuals making up the team are complementary in their individual strengths and weaknesses. Learning systems and practices are also organized in such a way that they recognize that different people have different learning styles and preferences. In short, spiritually based organizations celebrate personal differences and diversity rather than shunning them.

Fear is a major demon plaguing many organizations, at both the individual and organizational levels. Individuals fear that they may lose their jobs as a result of the growing culture of restructuring and downsizing. Organizations fear the turbulence and uncertainty in the task environment.

Fearful people cannot maximize their potential. A strong belief in and devotion to the organization's vision and mission is a key way to reduce fear in an organization. If people are consciously and truly committed to the vision and the mission and they are doing whatever it takes to realize the vision and accomplish the mission, that organization is immortal until its mission is accomplished. If individuals are doing all they can and they are doing the right thing to ensure organizational success, they have no reason to fear—the organization will retain them. If it won't, they can be assured that "no truly great man or woman can complain of lack of opportunities." It may only be a matter of time.

An organization that has created the climate described above creates what Rick James (2004) calls "space for grace." It is in this space that organizational miracles can happen. It is in this stage that the synergy between reason and faith or intuition can be maximized. I remember one such miracle in an organization I was working in. We hired a consultant to do an end-of-program evaluation and to help resolve a deep conflict between staff on one hand and management and the board on the other. He was given a 50-day contract. In my assessment, he was a spiritually based consultant who believed in integrating reason and intuition. After five days he surprised all of us. He said, "After listening to all of you, intuitively I can put my finger on the main issues in terms of the performance of your program and the conflict you are going through. I can produce the report in three days and go back home. However, if you still want me to hang around for the 50 days you have allocated, I would be happy to spend them as a holiday in your country, and besides, I need the money too." He did the work in 10 days and went back home. He was paid for the 10 days.

The challenge of human progress

Deep developmental work cannot avoid engaging in spiritual warfare or the war between good and evil. This leaves the reason only-based individual largely ineffective, as she cannot consciously engage at this level of the struggle. Vices like corruption, bribery, oppression, greed, double standards, deep-seated poverty, and selfishness, among many others, have their roots in the spiritual dimension and may only be dealt with fundamentally at that level. Forces of evil will usually rise up to undermine genuine developmental work. Without spiritual power, we may be dealing with symptoms rather than the root causes.

If there is a devil who personifies evil and he is a wise being, then he must target his warfare on the centers of power. The war between evil and good is likely to concentrate on political centers, economic centers, institutions of higher learning; centers of religion, media, and entertainment. These are the centers of power in the world. The constant question is who is controlling these centers of power, what is their agenda, and what values are they promoting? What spiritual forces and pressures are good people in these centers facing in their effort to build a better world for all? And how able are they to help the individuals and groups in these organizations identify, surface, and confront their contradictions for change for good? How much power do these change agents have, and how can they cultivate their spiritual power for more and deeper effectiveness?

As long as evil exists in the world, perfect utopia cannot be attained. This is a call for vigilance to put evil at bay as much as we can. Once we slack off, evil creeps back to reclaim the space it had been pushed from. If the feeling of struggle against evil ceases among the people, the individual, community, organization, or country, their spirituality is probably in a state of decay. Struggle and striving are signs of positivity and pursuit of good. Perfect utopia cannot happen because it would mean that evil has ceased to exist. Perfect oblivion on the other hand would mean that evil has triumphed over good. Utopia will always be in the future because it is progress in the triumph over evil rather than a destination.

It is times of crisis that expose the children of light and the children of darkness. In a moment of choice, one cannot be neutral. Spiritual people are willing to sacrifice their self-interest for the sake of promoting good. Where one stands in the moment of choice must always be clear. In the words of C.S. Lewis, "There is no neutral ground in the universe. Every square inch, every split second is claimed by God and counterclaimed by Satan." We cannot stand in the middle, between God and Satan. Not to choose is a choice to stand with evil.

Reversals in development are possible especially if there is a slackening of consciousness at higher or spiritual levels. A broader consciousness about the real nature of problems is necessitating the integration of reason and faith and the need to give spirituality more space to more consciously contribute toward human progress. Personal and organizational change efforts will never reach their full potential without the conscious rediscovery of the human spirit.

BIBLIOGRAPHY

Adair, J., 2002. *Effective Strategic Leadership*. Macmillan: London.
Belkin, M., 1988. *Introduction to Counseling*. Wm. C. Brown Publishers: Dubuque, Iowa.
Biko, S., 2006: *I Write What I Like*. Pilcador Africa: J'burg
Block, P., 1996. *Stewardship: Choosing Service over Self-Interest*. Berrett-Koehler Publishers: San Francisco.
Buber, M., 1987. *I and Thou*. T&T Clarke Ltd.: Edinburgh.
Bryne, R., 2006. *The Secret*. Atria Books: New York.
Canfield, J., 2007. *How to Get from Where You Are to Where You Want to Be: The 25 Principles of Success*. Harper Element: London.
Carson, C., (ed), 1998. *The Autobiography of Martin Luther King, Jr*. Warner Books: New York.
Carr, W., 1991. *Manifold Wisdom: Christians in the New Age*. SPCK: London.
CDRA, 2003. *Seeing the Eye of the Needle*. CDRA: Cape Town.
CDRA, 2004. *Emergence-From the Inside Out*; CDRA: Cape Town.
Collins, G., 1969. *Search for Reality*. Key Publishers: Wheaton, Illinois.
Covey, S., 1991. *Principle-Centered Leadership*. Simon & Schuster Company: London.
Covey, S. & R. Merrill, 1994. *First Things First: Coping with the Ever-Increasing Demands of the Workplace*. Simon & Schuster: London.
Covey, S., 2004. *The 8th Habit: From Effectiveness to Greatness*. Simon & Schuster: New York.
Drucker, P., 1990. *Managing the Non-Profit Organization*. Butterworth-Heinemann: London.
Eyben, R., 2011. "Relationships Matter: The Best Kept Secret of International Aid?" in *An Annual Digest for Practitioners of Development*, CDRA: Cape Town.
Fischer, L., 1997. *The Life of Gandhi*. HarperCollins: London.
Frankl, V., 1986. *The Doctor and the Soul*. Vintage Books: New York.
Fuller, Buckminster R., 1969. *Oblivion or Utopia: The Prospects for Humanity*. Bantam Books: London.
Gardner, H., 1995. *Leading Minds: An Anatomy of Leadership*. HarperCollins Publishers: London.
Handy, C., 2006. *Myself and Other More Important Matters*. Arrow Books: London.
Hanson, P & B. Lubin, 1995. *Answers to Questions Most Frequently Asked About Organization Development*. Sage Publication: London.
Harrison, R., 1995. *The Collected Papers of Roger Harrison*. McGraw-Hill: Berkshire, England.
Harvard Business Review., 2006. *Classic Drucker*. Harvard Business Publisher Corporation: Boston, Massachusetts.
Havel, V., 1990. The Revolution Has Begun, *Time* (March 5, 1990): 14 -15
Hill, N., 1966. *The Law of Success*. Master Mind Books: Bangalore.
———. 2003. Think and Grow Rich. Vermilion: London.
Hodgson, G., 2009. *Martin Luther King*. Quercus: London.
Hyde, M. & M. McGuiness, 2005. *Introducing Jung*. Totem Books: Lanham, Maryland.
James, R., 2004. *Creating Space for Grace: God's Power in Organizational Change*. Swedish Mission Council.
———. 2010. "Managing NGOs with Spirit" in *NGO Management: The Earthscan Companion*, Earthscan: London.
———. 2012. *Inspiring Change: Integrating Faith into Organization Development*. Digni: Oslo.
Kaplan, A. 1996. *The Development Practitioner's Handbook*. Pluto Press: London.

Kehoe, J. 1997. *Mind Power into the 21st Century.* Zoetic Inc: Vancouver.

Malunga, C., 2009. *Understanding Organizational Leadership through Ubuntu.* Adonis-Abbey Publishers: London.

Mandela, N., 2010. *Nelson Mandela: Conversations with Myself.* Macmillan: London.

Mansfield, S., 2005. *Derek Prince: A Biography.* Charisma House: Florida.

Maxwell, J., 2008. *Leadership Gold: Lessons I have Learned from a Life of Leading.* Thomas Nelson: Nashville.

Moreau, A, 1997. *Essentials of Spiritual Warfare.* Harold Shaw Publishers: Wheaton, Illinois.

Munroe, M., 2005. *The Spirit of Leadership.* Whitaker House: New Kensington.

Murphy, J., 2006. *The Power of Your Subconscious.* Mind Pocket Books: London.

Msafiri (the Traveller), November-December, 2011, Ed 78.

Nee, W., 1967. *Release of the Spirit.* New Wine Press, Chichester: England.

———. 1992. *The Spiritual Man.* Living Stream Ministry: California.

Orman, S., 2000. *The 9 Steps to Financial Freedom: Practical and Spiritual Steps So You can Stop Worrying.* Three Rivers Press: New York.

Peale, N., 1998. *The Power of Positive Thinking.* Vermilion: London.

Peck, M. Scott, 1997. *The Road Less Traveled and Beyond: Spiritual Growth in an Age of Anxiety.* Rider: London.

Phillips, D., 1998. *Martin Luther King, Jr. on Leadership.* Warner Books: New York.

Prince, D., 1987. *Spiritual Warfare.* Whitaker House: New Kensington.

Robbins, A. 1997. *Awaken the Giant Within.* Simon & Schuster: London.

Schuller, R., 2001. *My Journey: From an Iowa Farm to a Cathedral of Dreams.* HarperCollins: San Francisco.

Senge, P., 1990. *The Fifth Discipline: The Art and Practice of the Learning Organization.* Currency and Doubleday: New York.

Senge, P., C. Scharmer, J. Jaworski, & B. Flowers, 2004. *Presence: Human Purpose and the Field of the Future.* The Society for Organizational Learning Inc: Cambridge, MA.

Smith, T., 2001. *John Stott: A Global Ministry,* Intervarsity Press: Illinois

Tarcher, Jeremy P., 2010. *Mind is the Master: The Complete James Allen Treasury.* Penguin: New York.

Taylor, H., 1987. *Hudson Taylor's Spiritual Secret.* Moody Press: Chicago.

Tracy, B., 1993. *Maximum Achievement.* Simon & Schuster Paperbacks: New York.

Washington, J., 1991. *The Essential Writings and Speeches of Martin Luther King Jr.,* HarperCollins: London.

Wheatley, M. 2010. *Perseverance.* Berkeley Foundation: Utah.

Wheatley, M. *So Far from Home,* forthcoming

Wilkinson, B., 1999. *30 Days to Experiencing Spiritual Breakthroughs.* Multnomah Publishers: Oregon.

Yancey, P., 2007. *Soul Survivor: How My Faith Survived the Church.* Hodder & Stoughton: London.

Zacharias, R. 1994. *Can Man Live Without God.* Word Publishing: Milton Keynes, England.

Index

driven process of, 95; lessons on, 61–64; moving beyond knowledge, 113; in OD, 7–8, 41; organizational elements of, 112–14; organizations creating climate of, 114–16; purposeful living with, 9–10; reasons for increasing, 3–4; relationships defined by, 1; in self-development, 85; service important in, 23, 114; service to humanity through, 70; student comments about courses on, 7–8; tangible influence of, 107–8; wisdom cultivated through, 97

spiritual people: are not perfect, 64; becoming, 47–49; God and fellowship with, 88–89; self-interests sacrificed by, 117; wisdom sought, 89

spiritual power, 53; faith in, 92; goals accomplished through, 86; humanities contribution from, 62–63; lasting legacy from, 62–63

spiritual warriors, 70

strategies, 99–100

student comments, 7–8

subconscious mind, 25–26

substantialist mode of thought, 49–50

success, 97, 100

supernatural wisdom, 26

support, 79

Taylor, Hudson, 63

theology, of Gandhi, 60

thinking, 33–34

thinking sessions, 90–91

Thurman, Howard, 54

too much knowledge obscures wisdom, 7

Tracy, Brian, 51

transcendence, 38

trust, 19–20, 114–15

truth, 59

Truth and Reconciliation Commission, 13

ubuntu, 1

unconscious stage, of spiritual development, 67

Understanding Organizational Sustainability through African Proverbs (Malunga), 85

universal mission statement, 113–14

University professor, 64

values, 98–99, 112

vegetarianism, 59

vernacular language, 82

vision-crafting process, 20, 112

Western governments, 50

Wheatley, Margaret, 34, 70

wife's responsibilities, 76–77

wilderness experience, 48

will, 30–33

wisdom: Africans promotion of, 85–86; knowledge obscuring, 7; listening in, 28–29; spirituality cultivating, 97; spiritual people seeking, 89; supernatural, 26

wise man marries the woman he loves proverb, 77

women, 78

world, 3, 64–65

Zacharias, R., 81

About the Author

Chiku Malunga is the first and leading Indigenous Wisdom Based Organization Development (IWBOD) writer. He holds a doctorate degree in Development Studies from the University of South Africa. He is currently the director of CADECO (Capacity Development Consultants), an organization that promotes African-centered organizational improvement models.

Malunga's other books include: *Understanding Organizational Sustainability through African Proverbs*; *Making Strategic Plans Work: Insights from African Indigenous Wisdom*; *Understanding Organizational Leadership through Ubuntu*; *Oblivion or Utopia: The Prospects for Africa* and *Power and Influence: Self-Development Lessons from African Proverbs and Folktales.*